PRIYA PARMAR AND HINDI KRINSKY

Critical Literacy
in English Literature

PETER LANG
New York • Washington, D.C./Baltimore • Bern
Frankfurt • Berlin • Brussels • Vienna • Oxford

Library of Congress Cataloging-in-Publication Data

Parmar, Priya, author.
Critical literacy in English literature / Priya Parmar, Hindi Krinsky.
pages cm. — (Critical praxis and curriculum guides; vol. 2)
Includes bibliographical references.
1. Literature—Study and teaching (Secondary)—United States.
2. Critical pedagogy—United States. 3. Multicultural education—United States.
I. Krinsky, Hindi, author. II. Title.
PN70.P37   807.1273—dc23   2012042562
ISBN 978-1-4331-1398-7 (paperback)
ISBN 978-1-4539-1023-8 (e-book)
ISSN 2166-1367

Bibliographic information published by **Die Deutsche Nationalbibliothek.**
Die Deutsche Nationalbibliothek lists this publication in the "Deutsche
Nationalbibliografie"; detailed bibliographic data is available
on the Internet at http://dnb.d-nb.de/.

The paper in this book meets the guidelines for permanence and durability
of the Committee on Production Guidelines for Book Longevity
of the Council of Library Resources.

To Nitu, with love
     — PP

To my grandmother, the late Mrs. Devorah Krinsky,
whose life serves as an inspiration to all who knew her.
     — HK

Critical Literacy
in English Literature

CRITICAL PRAXIS AND CURRICULUM GUIDES

Shirley R. Steinberg and Priya Parmar

Series Editors

Vol. 2

The Critical Praxis and Curriculum Guides series
is part of the Peter Lang Education list.
Every volume is peer reviewed and meets
the highest quality standards for content and production.

PETER LANG
New York • Washington, D.C./Baltimore • Bern
Frankfurt • Berlin • Brussels • Vienna • Oxford

Contents

CHAPTER ONE

Introduction

The War on Public Schools and Literacy

High school is a place where work is done
All work no play, no time for fun.
I travel an hour just to get here
I stay for six hours and get nowhere.
And every week there's a test to take
But when it's done, I have plans to make.
There are so many rules about what not to do
How is chewing gum even bothering you?
And then there are people in the school
They come here, don't work, and act a fool.
But I'm "told" that I'm not a person with the right to complain
So sometimes I take school as just a game . . .
— by Laron (tenth grader, Brooklyn, NY)

The teacher talks about reality as if it were motionless, static, compartmentalized, and predictable. Or else [s]he expounds on a topic completely alien to the existential experience of the students. His [or her] task is to "fill" the students with the contents which are detached from reality, disconnected from the totality that engendered them and could give them significance. Words are emptied of their concreteness and become a hollow, alienated, and alienating verbosity. (Freire, 1970/2000, p. 53)

The changing demographics of North American school children is raising new challenges for educators, specifically on how to address the cultural and linguistic needs of all students to ensure that they will achieve academic success. Are educators standing up to the challenge? What other obstacles are educators facing and how can we deal with them most effectively?

According to the opinion of Laron (pseudonym used to pro-
tect student's identity), a tenth-grade student attending high
school in Brooklyn, the answer to the first question posed above is
a resounding "no." Laron's feelings of traveling one hour to school
only to be met with mundane, test-driven, rule-bound, and mech-
anistic routines are common experiences shared by many students
who attend schools that are technocratic and positivist in nature.
Sadly, the experiences Laron described are not new or improved.
Decades ago, Brazilian educator, philosopher, and activist Paulo
Freire described a reductionist approach to education that pushes
teachers to use their time "wisely" and "efficiently" in a way that
forces rote learning, memorization, and mindless review of skills.
Curricula are often reduced to teaching decontextualized content
that is rendered meaningless and boring. Students, too, are reduced to mere objects, with no voice, decision making, or ownership in their own learning. As Laron declares: "But I'm 'told' that
I'm not a person with the right to complain."

The students who are not acting out due to boredom sit passively, trained to behave according to a set of rules and standards
that ultimately produce compliant, complacent citizens with skills
and behaviors that do not help them be active in a vibrant democracy or compete in the twenty-first-century job market. Due to
advancements in technology and the fast-changing job market,
it's crucial that public schools prepare students with the necessary
academic skills to equip them for higher education, or at the very
least, with marketable skills needed to enter the workforce imme-
diately upon graduating high school. However, due to the current
economic crisis, schools must re-examine how to best prepare *all*
students to pursue the path of higher education upon graduation.
According to the U.S. Bureau of Labor Statistics, as of April 2011
there was a 9.7 percent unemployment rate for high school graduates with no college education (slightly higher than the overall
9.2 percent unemployment rate) as compared to only 4.5 percent
unemployment rate for those with a bachelor's degree. The economic recession has made it uncertain if and when these statistics
will improve. Looking at the number of young people enrolled
in degree-granting institutions (including two-year colleges), females have continued to have higher numbers of enrollment than
males since 1980. According to the U.S. Department of Labor,
74 percent of female high school graduates entered institutions
of higher education compared with 66 percent males in 2009.
In addition to gender, the racial gap between African American
and White students persists with African Americans comprising
13.1 percent of college enrollees compared to 64.4 percent as of
the 2007–2008 academic year (Institute of Education Sciences,

2011). This gap is even greater between Hispanic students (11.4 percent) and White students (ibid.).

How can we improve, or work within, the current educational environment if we expect to improve these numbers and guide our students to compete globally? How do we go about providing democratic education where the goal is to create a civically minded intellectually productive society that is prepared for the job market changes and challenges of the twenty-first century?

The United States' Report Card

A brief look at current educational statistics of how U.S. school-aged children are performing, both internationally and nationally, will offer insight into how current educational reform efforts are faring. Internationally, the United States is ranked 18th among 36 industrialized nations in high school graduation rates, with 75–76 percent of high school students graduating on time (Weisburgh, 2007; United Press International, 2008). According to a 2011 report from the National Center for Education Statistics, the four-year graduation rate starting at the ninth grade of U.S. high school teenagers in academic year 2007–2008 was approximately 74.7 percent (Institute of Education Sciences, 2011).

When compared to other nations focusing on specific content areas, the United States has much catching up to do. According to the 2009 Programme for International Student Assessment (PISA) report, which assesses knowledge and skills of over 470,000 15-year-olds from 70 countries, the United States, when compared to 34 Organization for Economic Co-operation and Development (OECD) countries, ranked 25th in math, 14th in reading, and 17th in science (*USA Today*, 2010). Although the United States has shown improvement, the scores continue to fall behind the consistently high-ranking countries of South Korea, Finland, Japan, Canada, and New Zealand. South Korea, for example, ranked first in math and reading, and third in science, with Finland placing first in science and second in math and reading, followed closely behind by Canada, which ranks third in reading and fifth in math and science (Shepherd, 2010).

Within the U.S. though state-by-state statistics vary, there is evidence of a national assault on urban education. This has resulted in a class-based educational system in which students from low-income or working-class families tend to perform more poorly than their suburban or wealthier counterparts. According to the *State of America's Children 2010* report conducted by the Children's Defense Fund, the following educational statistics from 2007–2009 paint a grim picture:

- The U.S. spends almost three times as much per prisoner as it does per public school pupil.

- American schools are re-segregating: 73 percent of Black students and 78 percent of Hispanic students are in predominantly minority schools.

- More than 60 percent of fourth-grade public school students are reading or doing math below grade level. Eighty-five percent of Black and 84 percent of Hispanic students are reading below grade level. In math, 85 percent of Black and 79 percent of Hispanic students are achieving below grade level.

- Black students are more than three times more likely than White or Asian/Pacific Islander and twice as likely as Hispanic students to be suspended from school.

Point of Reflection

How do you negotiate or reconcile your curricular objectives and teaching philosophy to meet national/state/local standards?

- 46 percent of Black high school students, 39 percent of Hispanic and 11 percent of White students attend the 2,000 "dropout factories" across our country, defined as schools from which less than 60 percent of the freshman class will graduate in four years with a regular diploma.

- Teachers in high-poverty schools are more likely to have less experience, less training, and fewer advanced degrees than teachers in low-poverty schools.

- While the Black/White high school completion gap for young people 25–29 has closed, the Black/White gap in college completion persists. Lifetime earnings for a college graduate are almost twice those of a high school graduate.
(Children's Defense Fund, 2011)

We beg the question again: Are U.S. P–12 schools meeting the needs of their students? Are school curricula changing to reflect the growing cultural and ethnic diversity of its student population? According to the statistics provided above, arguably, the answer to both of these questions is a resounding no. Multicultural and culturally responsive teaching practices have taken a backseat to more pressing, and in our opinion, misguided, educational reform efforts, namely No Child Left Behind Act of 2001 enacted by former President George W. Bush. NCLB has, unfortunately, placed extreme pressure on schools and teachers to measure student performance by enforcing narrow and biased assessment measures—high-stakes standardized testing. NCLB was renewed, with slight changes, by President Barack Obama. The current administration goes a step beyond NCLB with the Race to the Top program which uses student scores on standarized tests to identify effective teachers and schools. This further stymies school curriculum and ecourages teaching to the test.

The Problems with High-Stakes Testing

Many public school teachers—and their students—as well as scholars and researchers in the field of education, believe that using high-stakes standardized tests as the *sole* measurement of academic achievement does not paint a fair or accurate picture of student learning because these assessments typically do not reflect higher-order thinking skills, individual intelligences, and creativity. Additionally, these exams, though now frequently used to measure effective teaching, are not a clear indicator of how skillful a teacher is at teaching.

We (Hindi and Priya) work closely with English high school teachers and both have experience teaching English at the secondary level: Hindi as a former English teacher, literacy coach, and college instructor, and Priya as a language and literacy (associate) professor at the City University of New York, Brooklyn College's School of Education, Secondary Education Department. Together, we solicited the opinions of New York City English teachers with whom we work closely. We frequently hear teachers' concerns about having to meet standards and preparing students for the test because the standards are "too standard" and static. Teachers complain of standards failing to acknowledge different ability levels or testing for *real* knowledge that would prepare students for the *real* world. They worry about standards focusing on low-level skills and the time constraints that encourage "teaching-to-the-test." Additionally, educators across the spectrum feel the punitive force of NCLB, the lack of resources that prevent them from meeting standards and the unfair pressure to meet the Annual Yearly Progress mandated by NCLB. In their own words:

> Standards are important but setting the bar at the same level for all students is not a good idea. Some students come to school at a *much* lower level and asking them to rise to the same standards is frustrating for them. I think the tests should be tiered based on a series of pre-assessments. Otherwise, it sets many of them up for failure. (Mrs. G, teaching 15 years, Brooklyn, NY)

> I know I must meet standards but doing so in the limited time I have prevents me from making my lessons meaningful. Another complaint, all the students are being challenged at the same level, which causes those who need extra help to fall behind and those who do well not to achieve to their fullest potential. (Ms. R, teaching 11 years, Brooklyn, NY)

It is burdensome to "teach to a test" that is not at all aligned to college readiness. Students come into high school largely unprepared. They are reading and writing well below grade level because [junior high school] teachers are forced to teach to the exam, which does not always prepare them for high school reading and writing. It is difficult to get them to grade level while also preparing them for college. (Ms. H, teaching 3 years, Brooklyn, NY)

Meeting standards and preparing my students for the state exams are difficult with all the activities and projects you *want* to assign to your students; it takes away from incorporating the topics you yourself believe are also crucial to enhancing a student's reading and writing. (Ms. G, teaching 19 years, Brooklyn, NY)

I am very frustrated by the state's decision to make testing a central part of the ELA curriculum—I know that students' knowledge must be evaluated, but testing can only account for a fraction of what students learn. I would also have to say that trying to instill a love of reading in the students while being constrained by a testing culture is my biggest challenge. I just try to stay creative and maintain my own enthusiasm for the literature in order for my students to become enthusiastic about it themselves. (Ms. D, teaching 11 years, Brooklyn, NY)

High-stakes testing, coupled with time constraints and limited resources, make it difficult for teachers to implement student-centered, project-based, contextualized lessons that could help bridge the gap between diverse populations of learners. Additionally, focusing exclusively on skills-based instruction decontextualizes learning, which is in contradiction to empirical educational research that has shown the effectiveness of incorporating multicultural and culturally responsive teaching and constructivist-based learning models (Ladson-Billings, 1992; Gay, 2000; Lee, 2001).

To complicate matters further, the objectivity of standardized tests has been called into question, specifically the cultural and class biases that some argue are embedded throughout the exams. Does the development of high-stakes exams account for the diverse cultural and linguistic population of students? Although test makers like Educational Testing Service have argued that racial, class, and gender biases have been removed from their exams, others remain skeptical (Crouse & Trusheim, 1988; Hood & Parker, 1989; PURE, 2007). In one incident, controversy arose after the following question appeared on a 2006 New York State Regents Exam: "What were two ways the British improved the lives of Africans?" The question followed a passage written in 1922 that concluded: "We are endeavoring [trying] to teach the native races to conduct their own affairs with justice and humanity, and to educate them alike in letters and in industry" (Rammohan, 2007).

Is this question racist? Inappropriately worded? Or, is it permissible because it is embedded within the study of imperialism, which is covered within social studies? According to the Chicago-based group Parents United for Responsible Education (PURE), the question is racially biased. This advocacy group contends that the Regents and other standardized exams continue to reflect biases against students of color, English-language learners, and low-income students, listing several other examples of bias in a "Fact-Sheet" report published in 2007 (PURE, 2007).

Another area of concern is that standardized exams treat all students as if they are academically the same. This myth of treating everyone the same or holding every student to the same standard raises some serious concerns because teachers are simultaneously required—and even evaluated on—their ability to differentiate their teaching to meet the needs of a diverse range of learners.

These issues of objectivity and bias become further pronounced when we look at who is performing well on these exams. Research indicates that high-performing students tend to come from middle- to high-income households, while low-performing students tend to come from lower-income households. Why is academic achievement class oriented? If teachers are teaching and holding every student to the same standard, shouldn't performance have zero relevance on socioeconomic class? Clearly, there is an underlying bias that must be addressed to allow for more equitable learning.

To better understand this class bias, we must question the objectivity of these tests. What specific questions and content are included in the exam? How are questions phrased or constructed? Who writes the questions? Which demographic of students are initially tested when creating the exams? How do we know questions will not be interpreted differently based on the students' cultural and linguistic backgrounds? How is the "correct" answer determined? What format—multiple choice, short essay—is chosen and why? The simple answer to these questions is that standardized testing measures, by definition, are not supposed to take into account socioeconomic status and cultural or linguistic diversity. The irony, however, is the word *standard*, which implies consistency; therefore, when standardized exams are administered, it is expected that interpretations of the questions and answers remain consistent too. Is this possible when working with students from diverse cultural, linguistic, and class backgrounds?

The unavoidable truth is that the construction of *any* exam involves human decision making. This piece of information alone should raise concerns of objectivity due to the mere fact that humans (test makers) are subjective beings who hold personal values, beliefs, and ideological positions that may influence the development of questions and answers. This being the case, we believe there is no such thing as a neutral or ideologically free exam.

In addition to the subjective nature of the exams, it is important to understand the pressure high-stakes testing puts on educators. In order to meet the demands instituted by state and government officials, some of whom have very little or no teaching experience, school administrators and teachers are faced with undue pressure to produce high test scores. These scores often result in teachers' teaching to the test, carving out entire school days to devote time solely to test preparation. Incentive programs, such as merit pay or performance-based assessment of teachers, place even more pressure on schools and teachers.

Not all schools have been able to cope with these unrealistic demands and pressures. Several teachers and administrators have been accused of exaggerating and embellishing test scores for either career advancement or to receive additional state or federal funding. A desperate few administrators have even resorted to cheating to prevent their school from being shut down or taken over by new staff. In one case, the Atlanta public-school system is currently under investigation for allegedly cheating on state exams. In this case, approximately 140–160 teachers and 38 principals across 80 percent of Atlanta's public elementary and middle schools are accused of engaging in a "culture of cheating" to meet state standards on the 2009 Criterion-Referenced Competency Tests that students were required to take. It is alleged that teachers were instructed to erase incorrect answers and fill in the correct answers on exam sheets. This is not an isolated incident. Other states such as New York, Washington, D.C., Texas, and California have also faced or are currently facing similar cheating allegations. As a result, high-stakes testing has become a seriously divisive issue in the current debate of educational reform.

In the state of New York, the English Regents Exam, a standardized test, is usually taken during the eleventh grade and focuses primarily on reading comprehension. Imagine the pressure tenth- and eleventh-grade English teachers face in preparing their students for this exam. It is administered three times a year and students must earn a minimum 65 percent to earn a regular high school diploma and a minimum 85 to receive the Regents diploma to graduate. Now imagine the following scenario:

The morning bell rings and 33 students slowly file in. Quietly, they find their seats as the teacher, Mr. R, takes attendance. This is Mr. R's first class of the day and he's already feeling stressed about it. Yesterday, he was informed by his supervisor that his students do not seem

---

Point of Reflection

Take a moment to reflect on all the issues we have addressed thus far: the changing demographic landscape coupled with rapid advancements in technology; a crippled economy that has compelled educators to re-evaluate how to best prepare students for the changing job market; the challenges teachers face in meeting educational standards; the controversy over whether standardized exams are biased based on class, culture, or language; and the pressures teachers and students face as a result of all the above. How do all these issues manifest in a typical high school English classroom? What does it feel like to be a teacher or a student operating amid all these forces every single day?

prepared for the Regents exam next week. He was told, quite force-fully, that he's got to "step it up," which means getting through several more units of vocabulary and reviewing comprehension strategies all week. After taking attendance, Mr. R asks his students to take out their homework, a vocabulary review sheet on yesterday's unit. He knows that he has very little time to spend on reviewing mistakes, so Mr. R asks students to calculate their own errors as he calls out the right answers. He notices that several students are not following along, but there's no time to slow down the pace. He must cover this work and move on. Still, Mr. R's worried because if his class scores poorly on the Regents it will reflect badly on him. In fact, the school is under so much pressure that it may even cost him his job. His students are predominantly African American and come from low-income and working-class families. More than half of his students are at least one to two reading levels behind grade level and there are three students whose first language is not English. Mr. R wipes his brow. In his heart, he knows it is unlikely that most of the students in this class will perform well next week, but what should he do? Most of them are really great kids with a lot of potential; he just can't keep them interested in these endless reviews and strategy sessions. Should he slow down or push on in hopes the higher-performing kids will carry those who get lower grades? He decides to push on and is briefly shocked by his judgment call. Since when has test performance indicated student value?

He moves on, asking students for their grades and recording them in his record book. Mr. R tries to regain everyone's attention by moving on to literature. The students have been assigned to read four chapters of Lord of the Flies *at home. As he begins the lesson, he notices that a few students do not even have books out. Mr. R is frustrated. Now he must waste precious class time inquiring where their books are. Students respond gruffly, angrily, and use the opportunity to proclaim their total disinterest in the material. Mr. R sighs. "What a mess," he thinks, disgusted with himself. In high school,* Lord of the Flies *was one of his favorite books, and now he can barely motivate ten students to read it. He doesn't blame them for finding his reading questions and comprehension strategies dull, but his hands are tied: he must prepare them for the upcoming Regents exam and this is what his supervisor wants him to do. As the students continue to groan, Mr. R inwardly groans with them. He wonders, "What's the point of all this, these spit-back drills and mechanical exercises? Why are we all wasting our time?"*

Point of Reflection

Reflect for a moment on Mr. R's dilemma. Can you relate to him? What would you do differently if you were in this situation? Reflect for a moment on this episode from the students' perspective. How do you think Mr. R's students feel about him as a teacher? What do you think could be done to make this class more functional and educational?

As emphasized earlier, high-stakes testing inflicts such intense pressure that besides outright cheating by changing exam answers, some states have resorted to lowering academic standards and passing grades from 75 percent to 42 percent (Saulny, 2005). Teachers have been replacing real curriculum, creative lesson plans, and innovative pedagogies with hours and hours of test preparation. A study conducted by *Education Week* reported that 79 percent of teachers surveyed reported spending "a great deal" or "somewhat" of their instructional time in preparing students for test-taking, and 53 percent responded the same when asked if they used state practice tests (McNeil, 2000). With the increased pressures of high-stakes testing, a national study reported "nearly seven in ten teachers reported feeling test-stress, and two out of three believed that preparing for the test took time from teaching important but nontested topics" (Manzo, 2001). Test-stress has caused many veteran teachers, some who have been recognized and awarded for their teaching skills, to leave the profession. Many have left the public-school sector and flocked to private schools where test-preparation and high-stakes testing are not the center of the curriculum (Goodnough, 2001).

As policymakers work on improving test scores, assessing teacher preparation programs, and introducing performance-based assessment of teachers, very little time is devoted to analyzing and developing curriculum that is not standardized or pre-packaged. Most mainstream curriculum reform efforts are data-driven, systematic, quick-fix or pre-packaged, focusing on student and teacher accountability and preparing students for standardized exams. These types of curricula tend to classify and standardize students while de-skilling teachers and reducing them to rote-bound teaching methods that are decontextualized and culturally irrelevant. Many of these programs not only frustrate teachers, they do not adequately meet the needs of students from culturally and linguistically diverse backgrounds.

For far too long, policymakers have been pursuing a quick fix to the numerous problems in the field of education. Standardized testing may be quantifiable, but it tells us nothing about the quality of education our students are receiving. This panacea is a broken pipe dream. We believe that there are no quick fixes in this field. Instead, research supports reform efforts that are complex, local, and nuanced. In order to really target the needs of a vast range of students, educators must create a responsible learning system that accounts for the multidimensional factors and interconnected components that contribute, encourage, and support successful student performance.

What Can I Do?

At this point, you may be wondering what you can possibly do in the current situation, or how you can get a teaching job that allows you to actually *teach* your students. We understand and empathize with teachers feeling frustrated, concerned, or outright scared of going against the directives of higher officials, especially if teaching styles, approaches, and philosophies differ. We understand the fear of being reprimanded or receiving poor evaluations. This is why we wrote this book. The first step in achieving change is to take action. Because state and federal officials are essentially dictating to educators—the real experts—how to teach, we must reach out to our legislators by calling, writing, emailing and visiting, demanding our voices be heard. Boycott, protest, or picket legislation or outside interest groups that work to enforce policies that work against the interests of students, parents, and teachers. Participate in community-based and national organizations that are already fighting against anti-teacher practices and educationally restrictive policies.

We must also be proactive in our teachers' unions, taking on leadership roles within the union and school setting. This cannot be emphasized enough. We understand that some unions have become so bureaucratic and politicized that members become cynical and estranged from union activity. We urge you not to succumb to cynicism and passivity. Act and create change if you are dissatisfied with your union; after all, they are collecting union dues from your paycheck, so make your dues work for you. Unite with colleagues and parents to form collectives; take on leadership roles within your union; work strategically and intelligently to penetrate the "powers" within. Remember, a union is only as powerful as its members. If you are unhappy with union leadership, rally, demand change, or vote them out. We understand these actions take time and commitment; we understand you are inundated with grading, reporting, teaching to the test, completing paperwork, creating lessons, attending meetings, managing students and their parents, and dealing with your own emotional turmoil that stems from this profession. But if change is to occur, it must occur from within, from those of us who know education, pedagogy, students, and the communities in which we teach.

As stated above, we understand that one person alone cannot change the system, nor are we suggesting you try. We do hope, however, that if united with fellow educators (P–12, college professors, and administrators), community members, parents, and students, we can change our classroom, our school, our community. We encourage you to collect, record, and report data of your students' performance using authentic assessments that you create on your own. Most teachers create alternative qualitative assessment measures in their everyday teaching anyway (informal or formative assessments). Why not document them? Informal assessments can be any of the following: hands-on projects that create an outcome or product; posters or collages; group presentations or role-playing; portfolios; visual arts, poetry, or theatrical performances; deconstructing—and then reconstructing—popular television shows, films, or news shows; multimodal and multimedia projects; production of documentaries or docudramas, public service announcements, commercials, or musical lyrics. The possibilities are endless. In the end, all of these assessment tools materialize into a product—developed through a process—that can be shown as evidence of acquiring high-order thinking skills and critical literacy while also meeting English Language Arts standards. The result will be contextualized teaching and learning; student engagement, enthusiasm, and *real* education; increased attendance; higher-order critical thinking and literacy skills; and improved performance on exams. Furthermore, research has proven that students who are engaged in student-centered and problem-posing or project-based learning have shown increased engagement in class, improvement in cooperative learning skills, increased attendance rates, and improved scores on standardized exams (Thomas, 2000; Edutopia, 2011).

We implore you to record data regarding your lesson plans and students work as evidence that factored into improved test scores and attendance records—two items, politically speaking, that administrators view as important. However, this entails teachers taking risks—calculated and strategic risks with the support of those listed above. In Chapter Two, we'll explore why risk-taking is necessary; without it, your job security may indeed be in jeopardy (as it is now), American students' performance levels will continue in their average or downward spiral (as they are now), and more importantly, we will have produced a generation of youth who will find it extremely difficult to navigate successfully and productively in our rapidly changing world (as they are now). We want to turn our attention and focus on the role, responsibilities, and other challenges that English teachers face.

English Language Arts: An Opportunity for Meaningful Learning

What are the expectations and responsibilities of the high school English teacher? The simple answer is to engage students in reading, analyzing, and comprehending diverse bodies of literature in hopes of creating joy and pleasure for reading both print and non-print texts. The more complete answer is that, as all teachers are aware, their instruction is informed by content standards developed to guide lessons that build knowledge and skills. While the Common Core State Standards have been adopted by most of the U.S., the standards we have chosen to include in this book have been developed jointly by the International Reading Association (IRA) and the National Council on Teachers of English

(NCTE). The twelve English Language Arts standards were written with the understanding that they are interrelated and seen as a whole to engage students in reading, writing, listening, speaking, viewing, and visually representing (NCTE, 2011). We include the complete list of standards in the "Guide to using the unit plans" preceding Chapter Four for your reference. Keep these standards in mind as we present critical-literacy questions and activities in Chapters Four through Seven.

While standards are designed to guide a lesson, they should not be the *actual* lesson. The main objectives of ELA instruction must lie far beyond comprehension skills. The teachers we work with strive to make literature come alive by helping their students relate to the narratives by understanding how the messages found within are related to their own and the larger world. This is great literature. This is what makes literature so important to our spiritual and emotion well-being. A powerful story can shift mountains within our inner-world, awaken a volcano of imagination, and completely open our senses to new experiences. Great stories have the capacity to change the world.

Yet as we recognize these lofty aspirations, what are some of the real challenges English teachers face each and every day? Along with our colleagues in math, strong emphasis and undue pressure has been placed on English teachers to improve their students' English Language Arts test performance. As noted earlier in this chapter, the United States ranks average in reading performance—not much to be proud of for an industrialized, first-world superpower country. Is the pressure of meeting standards through high-stakes testing contributing to the dismal rankings? The short answer is yes, we believe so.

Many nationally accredited teacher-preparation programs across the nation are graduating teacher candidates with the knowledge, skills, and disposition that prepare them to teach in creative, innovative, and process-oriented ways. However, their passion and energy to teach is soon thwarted when they enter school districts that force them to discard all the creative efforts of designing student-centered, project-based, experiential learning strategies, and replace them with pre-packaged programs or teaching-to-the-test instructional methods. The disconnect between schools of education (teacher-prep programs) and public school districts is disconcerting. The teachers we work with, particularly in-service teachers (graduate education majors), make comments such as: "The lessons I created in my college courses were creative and thought-provoking, but unfortunately, they have no relevance in my real classroom because I'm forced to teach to the test"; or "The ideas I learn about in my graduate classes are great—fun, student-centered, meaningful—but I have to teach a specific

Point of Reflection

What are some challenges you face as a high school English teacher? Or, if you're not yet a teacher, what are some of your concerns or fears? Take a few moments to reflect and share your thoughts with a colleague or mentor.

model [pre-packaged curriculum], otherwise, I'll get in trouble from my principal."

The Realities of the ELA Classroom

What are some other challenges high school English teachers are faced with beyond pressures of preparing students for exams? Our colleagues in high schools report one of their biggest frustrations is simply getting their students interested in reading and comprehending texts, especially print texts.

> My biggest challenge is teaching students the enjoyment of literature. I often feel as if we are making the art of reading "work" for them. We have lost the appreciation of a book for pleasure. I also think we should encourage discussion of literature, which is not always possible due to time constraints and packed curriculum. If we can get kids to like reading, the rest would come naturally. (Ms. P, teaching four years, Brooklyn, NY)

> I would have to say that the biggest challenge is grabbing the attention of the students when we're discussing literature in class. Some students already come to class with preconceived notions that they cannot possibly enjoy or be interested in a book that we read as a part of English class. In other words, trying to keep the students interested and actively participating in the class takes a great deal of effort and can often be a challenge as it is with any other teacher for any other subject. (Mrs. D, teaching 19 years, Brooklyn, NY)

With the advancement of technology, ELA teachers must also contend with the changing literacy landscape, specifically the advent of videogames, iPhones, iPods, texting, Twittering, blogging, YouTube, or social networking sites like Facebook. In this digital era, teachers are encouraged (or forced) to create interactive classrooms by using the latest technologies available—SMARTboards, Mimios Boards, and computers. We are not opposed to the use of technology; in fact, we believe it should be whole-heartedly embraced by the educational community. The problem, we feel, is that most teachers do not receive adequate training on how to use these technologies in really innovative ways. Many teachers simply substitute the blackboard and pencil for the SMARTboard and keyboard (Adams & Petty, 2003). This frustration with being unable to use technology properly, we believe, creates feelings of resentment and fosters a resistance to these new media forms.

> The biggest issue facing the English teacher today is technology, particularly videogames. The games make it almost impossible to reach students who are lost in their virtual worlds. Often times, teachers have to make connections to the text with a

game or a movie or a texting code in order for the students to visualize. (Mrs. G, teaching 15 years, Brooklyn, NY)

I feel the biggest issue ELA instructors face today is the constant force of technology that is pushed on us. It is difficult to keep up with how fast things change. Teachers can only use so much technology in a day. Sometimes we don't even have the resources to keep up with such advances or if we do, some teachers need to be trained on how to use it! Intense preparation is needed to fully experience the full potential of technology. (Mr. C, teaching one year, Brooklyn, NY)

Chapter Three will explore the importance of understanding youth culture and incorporating their literacies— popular culture, media, and digital texts—into the planning of our lessons. We will also discuss the challenges associated with the new media forms, including lack of resources, large class sizes, and students entering high school woefully unprepared to tackle the most basic literacy tasks.

We hope to alleviate some of the challenges quoted above by providing critical-literacy activities (discussed in depth in Chapter Two) that will cultivate an interest, even joy, in reading and writing while also developing deep-level analysis as promulgated by a critical pedagogy. Although we find standardized testing to be problematic, we hope to help you meet the standards and prepare students to perform well on these exams by incorporating critical literacy. While our primary goal is to promote critical literacy, it is important for teachers to understand that in the process of incorporating critical literacy, students learn to be "critical," or in other words, they become conscious and aware, questioning, analyzing, deconstructing, and reconstructing seemingly normal, "fixed" policies and practices, traditions, and ideological beliefs as malleable.

Student Voices in the ELA Classroom

Up to this point, we have been focusing on the responsibilities and challenges facing the English teacher. We have read and reflected on some of their concerns. But what do *students* think about school? How do they feel about reading? Do they like what they are doing in their English literature class? We conducted a small study surveying 60 ethnically diverse students attending various Brooklyn high schools. We were interested in their feelings about school in general and then focused our questions on targeting their reading habits and experiences in English literature. When asked if they like school, responses were an overwhelming yes: 90

percent of students like school. Below are a few of responses that reflect the majority's sentiments:

> I like going to school. I can make a lot of friends in school, as well as grasping new knowledge. Being in a school setting allows me to enhance my reading skills as well as broaden my view. (female, tenth grade)

> I do like school, but sometimes I feel that the curriculum is dull and boring and a lot of stuff we learn is stuff we can't use in real life. For example, with English class we read the same traditional and dated material that everyone has been reading for decades; in my Social Studies class we learn about the government but we are not told how we can implement this knowledge to become active or involved in politics to further our education. (female, eleventh grade)

> Yes, I like school because most of the classes I am taking now are preparing me for college and I get a feel of what college is going to be like. (female, twelfth grade)

The percentage of students expressing a dislike of school commented on the stress of taking exams, boring or difficult topics, and having to get up early.

When asked if students liked their English literature class, the vast majority (80 percent) responded yes, citing they enjoyed engaging in group discussions, debates, project-based activities, role-playing scenes of the book, re-writing the book, and creating lyrics or other media texts from the themes reflected in the books. They also expressed enjoying novels that they could relate to as opposed to the "old, boring" novels, which they found difficult to visualize while reading.

> My favorite part is the discussion where we are put into groups of four, with partners assigned by the teacher and not necessarily the same groups every time. And then we get to discuss for approximately five to ten minutes. The reason I like it is because while sharing my ideas, I get to listen to different opinions and point of views that I find interesting and sometimes never even considered before. (female, twelfth grade)

> I like reading novels and being assigned fun projects, especially group projects. (male, ninth grade)

> My most favorite project was a cookbook I made based on the foods in a book. We were allowed to work in groups but I decided to work alone and presented it . . . and I got a 100% on it! (female, tenth grade)

> I love when we do projects after reading a book. My favorite assignment was when we had to read a book then make a soundtrack for the book. So for example we had to choose six scenes in the book and we would have to choose a song for each of the scenes that described the scene the most. Then we had to choose a verse or lines in the song that described the scene and why we chose the song . . . (male, eleventh grade)

> Illustrating or acting out scenes. Always fun to do and watch (male, ninth grade)

What they like least is writing essays, reading aloud, responding to "question-answer" type worksheets, and as noted above, reading old, outdated books.

> I dislike that we have to read old and dated books like the ones that Shakespeare wrote. Why do we focus on so many of his books? Why can't we learn about stuff that is interesting or read about people from the twenty-first century? (female, eleventh grade)

> In my English class my least favorite activity is the long essays we have to write when we finish reading a book we were assigned to read. (male, ninth grade)

> My least favorite assignment is when we have to write short answer responses to questions after reading a book. Most of the time, I don't find the answer immediately. The pace of the class moves too fast. I need more time to take in the story in order to answer the short responses correctly. (female, tenth grade)

> My least favorite assignment is when we go over vocabulary after reading a book. Since there are about 20 words we have to know, we have to make 20 flash cards that include writing the definitions, synonyms, definition in your own words, and a sentence using the word. (female, ninth grade)

Point of Reflection

If you are a teacher, ask your students to give constructive feedback on your curriculum and class activities. Which aspects do they most enjoy? Which do they least enjoy? Why? How will their feedback affect your instruction? Or, if you are not yet a teacher, gain insight by asking a teenager her/his opinion of English literature classes.

While we were thrilled to learn that most students in our study enjoyed their English literature class, we were not too surprised to learn that most (90 percent) of these same students enjoyed reading for pleasure; however, of the texts they enjoyed reading, most were unlikely to ever appear in the ELA curriculum: contemporary novels, graphic novels, sci-fi zombie books, magazines, online newspapers, and blogs.

Part of successful teaching includes asking for constructive feedback from our students. The more they are engaged in the learning and decision-making process, the more success you will have in teaching them to read, write, and participate in classroom activities and discussions.

As we have expressed throughout this chapter, we understand teachers are busy. We also recognize the realities teachers face each day and the challenges that are involved in creating individual curriculum units within the current positivist educational framework. In interviews we have conducted with teachers in high-needs schools, we know that many teachers are facing limited time, lack of resources, overcrowded classrooms, and now, the pressures of high-stakes testing and accountability (performance-based assessment of teachers). We recognize that it is not easy to be a teacher in today's public schools.

Despite all the hardships you face, we applaud you for pursuing your dream. We thank you in advance for your service and hope this book offers some helpful tips and ideas to make your time as a teacher enjoyable and rewarding. Research suggests that teachers need to have well-designed, thematic-centered curricula and lessons at their disposal (Quint, 2006). This is accomplished when the school works as a community to meet its own needs. Community in this sense includes working collaboratively with students, parents, and local community organizations to help build the curriculum. Practically, this means that time is devoted to professional-development workshops, not exam reviews or test-preparation pointers, but real learning. Together with administrators, teachers form professional learning communities (PLCs) to discuss, analyze, and revise curricula and share pedagogical strategies that meet the needs of their particular school demographics. This communal approach was found to be more successful than requiring each individual teacher to create lessons on his or her own (ibid.).

> **Point of Reflection**
>
> Reflect on your growth as an educator. What changes do you hope to make in your professional life? How do you plan to incorporate some of these ideas in your own practice?

Ideally, we would love it if each teacher could create his or her own authentic lessons because only you truly know your students. We encourage this, because it is possible. However, as educators ourselves, we understand the realities our colleagues in public high schools face, especially when teaching in urban areas. This primer is written as a guide and resource for English teachers to use, expand upon, revise, and be inspired by. It bridges sound theory with practice and seeks to give you the pedagogical tools with which to operate in a high-stakes environment while being an agent of change and an effective teacher. The appendix contains reproducible printable guides for teachers to use or edit if teaching any of the featured novels we focus on in Chapters Four through Seven.

In writing this primer, we were inspired and informed by our fellow high school English colleagues, novice and experienced, and the youth we work with. A number of beliefs form the foundation of the primer. First, we believe that we must set high expectations for all of our students if we expect them to succeed. Second, we believe that all teachers need to be well informed about the cultures in which their students operate, and connect recent cultural developments with ideas of diversity and multiculturalism by incorporating them with innovative, calculated, risk-taking pedagogies. Third, we believe that it is essential to use innovative pedagogies in preparing students to pass mandated, standards-based, high-stakes exams. Based on sound research, theory, and equally important, our own experiences as secondary English teachers and working with pre- and in-service teacher candidates, we believe that it is possible to teach literature in a manner that is not only academically focused, but also culturally and contextually relevant and personally meaningful.

CHAPTER TWO

Counter-War Approach

Critical Literacy

Mis-educated

What is it that they are trying to keep from us?
Is it the fact that they lied to us?
The use of books that hold fiction
by telling us Christopher Columbus discovered this land?
And silence us on other parts of history, like
where the Native Americans came in?
I wonder something:
Did we ever get credit for what we created?
When you look in every book
They have a white man holding a poster
Talking about "we the people are a nation."
When push comes to shove we stand alone
Where's our black fathers who founded
The stuff we use today?
Mis-educated is what we are today.
No idea of who created the telephones
Or where did our mothers get their irons from
They tell us nothing, nothing at all!
That's why we're mis-educated . . .
Mis-educated to the world!
— by Janaisha (tenth grader, Brooklyn, NY)

To acquire literacy is more than to psychologically and me-
chanically dominate reading and writing techniques. It is to
dominate these techniques in terms of consciousness; to understand what one reads and to write what one understands; it is
to *communicate* graphically. Acquiring literacy does not involve
memorizing sentences, words, or syllables—lifeless objects un-
connected to an existential universe—but rather an attitude

of creation and re-creation, a self-transformation producing a stance of intervention in one's context. (Freire, 1973, p. 48)

Teaching English from a *critical* perspective moves beyond the traditional canon to include alternative and subjugated texts. These kinds of texts prompt students to draw multiple meanings and interpretations based on their own personal histories and experiences. Scholar, educator, and activist Paulo Freire expresses it beautifully in the above quote where he encourages educators to rethink and reconceptualize what it means to teach literacy to our students. Critical literacy is designed to equip students with the tools and skills necessary to achieve beyond academic standards. In other words, critical literacy transcends academic expectations by inspiring student *agency* outside the confines of the classroom walls and into their social, political, and economic worlds. As we will remind you several times throughout this book, critical literacy is not a technique, a method of teaching, or the act of acquiring reading and writing skills in a decontextualized manner. We again refer to Freire's quote in the epigraph to reinforce the notion that critical literacy is a consciousness, "an attitude of creation and re-creation" of self-awareness and transformation. Approaching literacy from this perspective requires educators to carefully self-reflect on their own educational philosophy and the perceptions and expectations they have of their students. This also includes a deep awareness and understanding of the political nature of the education system within the context of society. Before examining critical literacy in more detail, we will first define literacy.

Defining Literacy

Point of Reflection

Take a moment to think about what literacy means to you. Reflecting on your own educational experiences, explain the process of learning literacy skills.

Over the past hundred years, our conceptualization of literacy and what it means to be literate has undergone numerous evolutions. At its most basic and simplistic form, literacy has been defined as the ability to read and write (Blake & Blake, 2005). Other definitions have also included the ability to spell, speak, and listen (i.e., those of the National Council of Teachers of English and the International Reading Association). The word *illiterate* is used to describe individuals who lack any reading or writing abilities, oftentimes referring to having received little to no formal education (Blake & Blake, 2005).

Perspectives of literacy and what it means to be literate have dramatically shifted in the past few decades. Critical researchers have come to understand that the reading process is much more than a list of cognitive abilities. The conventional view of literacy as "a neutral set of skills that we have in our heads and

Point of Reflection

How do you define literacy? How does reading and writing play an integral role in your life? What literacies do you engage in outside of school?

develop through language teaching and learning" (Pahl & Rowsell, 2005, p. 3) has been consistently challenged and expanded. The traditional autonomous model that treats literacy as a neutral technology has been rejected by critical pedagogues in favor of an "ideological model" that defines literacy in association with its larger sociocultural contexts, ideologies, and purposes (Street, 1993; Blake & Blake, 2005). This new understanding redefines text as artifact or "objects with a history and . . . a material presence" (Pahl & Rowsell, 2005, p. 27).

Today, our notion of reading is postmodern in sentiment, multidimensional in thought, and accounts for cognitive skills, aesthetics, and sociocultural contexts (Alexander & Fox, 2004). New educational research asserts that literacy is a socially constructed and socially negotiated phenomenon and "reading and writing can only be understood in the context of the social, cultural, political, economic, [and] historical practices . . . of which they are a part" (Lankshear, 1996, p. 210). In other words, literacy is much more than a list of psychological skills; it is a window into a complex and larger story. Despite this new research, schools today are experiencing a regression as educational policy pushes a standards-based framework shaped by older research models. This counter-trend, referred to by some as the "Era of Reconditioning," concentrates on "reading subskills and components [and] is less driven by theory than by other forces" (Alexander & Fox, 2004, p. 55). These forces, largely political, reject current research in favor of an older and more quantifiable understanding of literacy.

Two noted critical researchers in the field, Lankshear and McLaren (1993), urge educators to embrace these new findings and make "a significant shift in their conceptual, theoretical, or practical orientation" (p. xiii). We agree. Despite the new research, literacy is oftentimes still taught in rote, mechanical, and an entirely skills-based process limited to the simple acquisition of reading and writing skills. But this is just a fraction of its potential. We believe that literacy is a mindset, a philosophy, an awareness that all of life is comprised of texts, an array of endless living books that must be read, analyzed, interpreted, deconstructed, and challenged. As living, breathing beings, we are all unique, vibrant texts with a story, embedded within an interwoven world of endless stories.

Though we encourage you to expand your notion of literacy, it is unfortunate that many educators continue to operate within a limited and limiting framework. More than a decade ago, national organizations such as the National Council of Teachers of English (NCTE) and the International Reading Association (IRA) put forth a vision of literacy, including their own definition of critical literacy with goals to redefine how literacy is taught in

American schools. Despite this, the focus still remains on basic, uncritical literacy skills, or getting students to achieve functional literacy. To be functionally literate means being capable of reading, writing, and comprehending basic information such as "mastering and memorizing grammatical rules or being able to complete required reports, forms," (Parmar, 2009, p. 21) applications, financial forms (e.g., balancing a checkbook or writing a check), or government forms. Why have teachers set the bar so low? Is this the level of literacy we want our students to acquire? Is this *real* proficiency when a student is simply functional in society? Is this the real purpose of education or is it just schooling?

We differentiate between the terms *education* and *schooling*, arguing that schooling involves pushing forward hegemonic, technocratic practices that produce passive and complying citizens that further the interests of ideologies reflective of the dominant culture. This form of instruction discourages students from asking questions or challenging textbooks and indoctrinates them to act in prescribed manners. Textbooks are used as tools to sell so-called truths, as the final authority on what is right and wrong, what is centralized and marginalized, or excluded altogether, and ultimately, what is valued and devalued (Parmar, 2009). From our perspective, and we hope yours too, these are not the goals of education. A true education is transformative, life-changing, liberating, and revolutionary. True education entails a critical pedagogy.

> **Point of Reflection**
>
> Reflect on your own educational experiences. Were you schooled or were you educated? Next, turn your attention to the state of education today. Is today's education system reflective of schooling or of education? Reflect with a partner or write down your thoughts and share with your colleagues.

Critical Pedagogy

Critical pedagogy is situated within the theoretical framework of critical theory. Critical theory is often included within the field of cultural studies. We provide a brief introduction of both cultural studies and critical theory so that the reader understands the theoretical background of critical pedagogy. Understanding the theoretical underpinnings that drive any style of pedagogy and teaching philosophy is important if educators wish to fight to change their working conditions. It is crucial to understand that every teaching practice we witness as educators is driven by some philosophical and theoretical doctrine. As introduced in Chapter One, the current educational system, in general, is driven by a positivist, technocratic teaching philosophy. The proof of this is the standardization of students through mandated, high-stakes testing enforced by the federal No Child Left Behind Act. The purpose of this book is to inspire you to counteract technocratic teaching methods by employing a critical pedagogy and critical literacy.

Cultural Studies

Cultural studies is an interdisciplinary, transdisciplinary, and counter-disciplinary approach to reality, the world, traditional disciplines, and knowledge itself and is often associated with the study of popular culture, youth culture, and other historically marginalized or excluded cultures made invisible by Western canonical studies (Aronowitz & Giroux; 1993 Grossberg, 1994; Kincheloe & Steinberg, 1998; Kincheloe, Slattery, & Steinberg, 2000). Synthesizing the new cultural studies and literacy approaches, Frechette (2002), citing the work of Willis (1977), argues that all cultural expressions can be defined as cultural texts. In this way, texts are much more than a printed essay or a short story to be analyzed in a Literature class; they are communicative artifacts that interact and engage in a variety of multimodal ways. This new definition of text includes but is not limited to videogames, advertisements, films, weblogs, instant messaging, emails, television shows, comic books, graphic novels, and music.

Scholars of cultural studies also recognize the hierarchy that separates the culture of "others" and ostensible "high" culture. High culture, often referred to as "Cultural capital" (a term coined by French sociologist Pierre Bourdieu in 1986), is a form of the "right" or proper culture signified in its spelling of a capital "C" for Culture. Cultural capital is defined as representing:

> . . . a set of social codes in which those people who were Cultured knew what were the right books to read, the proper ways to interact at social gatherings, the proper forms of dress, the holiest manner to worship god, the correct modes of speech, and the proper culinary tastes . . . . The people, often referred to condescendingly as "the masses," who did not understand or share these sanctioned values possessed their own social codes, but these codes did not have the same power and therefore the same weight in society to persuade or influence opinions (Weaver, 2009, p. 1).

We urge educators to be conscious of Bourdieu's concept of Cultural capital because only then can culture be understood in terms of power and knowledge, embedded within social, historical, theoretical, and political frameworks, and operating both within and outside of our schools (Bourdieu & Passeron, 1990). Cultural studies scholars are concerned with how certain cultures, texts, knowledge, and representations are produced, reproduced, and appropriated within power structures (Aronowitz & Giroux, 1993; Lankshear & McLaren, 1993; Grossberg, 1994; Kellner, 1995; Kincheloe & Steinberg, 1998). Cultural studies scholars reject this hierarchical understanding and define culture as multidimensional and something that exists well beyond the study of societies, ethnic groups, and human civilizations (Parmar, 2009). This new definition sees culture as negotiable, pluralistic, hybrid, complex, and in a state of constant evolution. Culture is used as a medium for social, cultural, linguistic, and political critique and transformation. We reject the notion that educators must teach students the "right" knowledge. Instead, we believe that teachers and students share the teaching process by contributing their cultural knowledge and mutual expertise to the education process.

If we incorporate the culture of our students into our lessons, then we must accept that the knowledge they bring with them is indeed valuable and worthy of study. With this in mind, we include the knowledge found within the study of mainstream dominant culture, popular culture, and youth culture as part of cultural literacy texts that are rigorously analyzed, studied, and incorporated as part of a critical pedagogy. We provide additional explanations of culture in the form of *cultural literacy* later in this chapter and discuss the influence of popular culture and youth culture in Chapter Three. We also explore the importance of knowledge and how it is constructed and shaped in the *critical pedagogy* section below. But first, we introduce you to a brief historical background of critical theory.

Critical Theory

Critical theory emerged from a critical and distinct moment in history when important political and historical transformations were taking place between World War I and World War II. The theory is often associated with the Frankfurt Institute for Social Research, founded in 1923 in Frankfurt, Germany, typically referred to today as the "Frankfurt School." Among its members is Max Horkheimer, who coined the term "critical theory" and became the school's director in 1930. Other notable members included Leo Lowenthal, Theodor W. Adorno, Erich Fromm, Walter Benjamin, and Herbert Marcuse, among others. Members of the Frankfurt School were initially concerned with analyzing bourgeois power structures rooted in Marxism. With Hitler's rise to power, the concerns of the Institute, many of whom were Jews, changed (Darder, Baltodano, & Torres, 2003). The interdisciplinary nature of these critical theorists was evident in their attempts to bring together the works and philosophies of others such as Karl Marx, Immanuel Kant, Max Weber, and Friedrich Hegel to name a few. Over time, these theorists became increasingly invested in addressing the following two needs:

1. The need to develop a new critical social theory within a Marxist framework that could deal with the complex changes arising in industrial-technological, postliberal, capitalist society; and

2. The need to recover the philosophical dimensions of Marxism that had undergone a major economic and materialistic reduction by a new Marxist orthodoxy. (Warren, 1984, cited in Darder, Baltodano, & Torres, 2003, p. 9)

Other influential theorists contributing to the development of critical theory are Italian revolutionary Antonio Gramsci, French philosopher and historian Michel Foucault, and German sociologist and philosopher Jürgen Habermas.

Inherently tied to critical theory is the act of resistance. Critical theory is concerned with hegemonic domination and power relations permeating institutions of power. What does this mean exactly? We have used the word *hegemonic* believe and use it frequently throughout the chapter. To better understand our position, it is important to discuss the definition of hegemony here before proceeding. Italian Marxist Antonio Gramsci coined the term and defined it as:

> [T]he permeation *throughout* society of an entire system of values, attitudes, beliefs and morality that has the effect of supporting the status quo in power relations. Hegemony in this sense might be defined as an "organizing principle" that is diffused by the process of socialization into every area of daily life. To the extent that this prevailing consciousness is internalized by the population, it becomes part of what is generally called "common sense" so that the philosophy, culture and morality of the ruling elite comes to appear as the natural order of things. (Burke, 1999, 2005, as cited in Parmar, 2009, p. 8)

Keeping this definition of hegemony in mind, critical theory is concerned with the effects of these power structures, specifically on those it oppresses in all dimensions of their lives, including economically, politically, and socially. Critical theory places heavy emphasis on the need for individuals to be politically aware of their social, economic, and educational contexts, as well as understanding how all these components are interrelated. This type of analysis necessitates the development of a theoretical framework that historically and socially situates the deeply embedded roots of racism, discrimination, violence, and disempowerment that manifest themselves in insidious forms. Instead of perpetuating the assumption that such realities are inevitable, critical theory invites individuals to explore the relationship between these larger historic, economic, and social constructs and their inextricable connection to ideology and power (Parmar, 2009).

We will now focus our discussion on how critical theory is practiced within the educational system. When we reject the hegemonic nature of schools, in favor of a more transformative, more just, and more equitable education system, we are enacting a critical pedagogy. We cannot talk about critical pedagogy without first paying homage to one of its most influential pioneers, Brazilian cultural worker, educator, philosopher, and social and political activist Paulo Freire.

Paulo Freire

As you have probably noticed, we start each chapter with a quote by Paulo Freire that reflects the chapter's content. Our work is inspired by Freire's commitment and passion for a truly democratic society and inclusive, equitable, education system in which students are not schooled, but educated. We admire the fact that Freire, in many of his writings, urges his readers to take nothing at face value, even to the point of challenging and questioning his theories. This is something we don't often hear from mainstream educators in P–12 schools and in higher education. Freire pushes the reader to go beyond his ideas, to accomplish more, and not idolize him as some sort of hero or superior being. In the spirit of Paulo Freire, we too, encourage you to question and challenge our words, understanding that our biases and ideological positions are intentionally made obvious throughout the book. We encourage you to add to, change, edit, and adapt our ideas to meet your classroom needs. We strongly advise you to be critical of *all* work in this way and to accept no one's words at face value, or as objective, or neutral.

A Brief Biographical Sketch of the Life and Work of Paulo Freire

Paulo Regulus Neves Freire was born on September 19, 1921, in Recife, Pernambuco, located in northeast Brazil, to a middle-class family. By reading to him, his parents were influential in sparking in him, at a very young age, a deep-rooted passion for the written word (McLaren, 2000). When world economic disaster struck in 1929, Paulo and his family were forced to move to Jaboatâo in 1931, located 11 miles from Recife. When Paulo was 13, his father died, he spent much of his free time with poor families and laborers who lived in rural areas (Gadotti, 1994, cited in McLaren, 2000). During this time, Paulo witnessed the experiences of the poor, what it was like to be hungry, and how poverty affected other areas in life, particularly academic performance. Paulo eventually returned to Recife to attend a private high school on a scholarship that his mother managed to secure. Paulo would also become the school's Portuguese language teacher while still a high school student himself. Later he went on to earn a law degree. At the age of 23, he married an elementary school teacher, Elza Maria

Costa Oliveira, who was instrumental in sparking Paulo's early interest in literacy (McLaren, 2000). Before her death in 1986, Elza and Paulo had five children together, three of whom later went on to become educators. In 1988, Paulo married his childhood friend, Ana Maria A. Hasche, whom he referred to as "Nita."

Freire's life and professional experiences shaped his passion for teaching literacy to marginalized and oppressed peoples. Rather than pursue a career in law, Paulo dedicated his life to public service, holding various directorial positions within the Social Service of Industry, a government agency set up to improve standards of living for workers and their families. He became its director of the Division of Education and Culture, and later, its superintendent. After holding several posts from 1956 to 1958, Paulo began teaching at the School of Fine Arts in Recife as professor of history and philosophy of education. Besides his childhood experiences playing with children from poor families, his professional experiences as a public servant brought Freire in direct contact with the poor throughout Brazil. This helped to shape his research while pursuing his doctorate degree, resulting in his thesis titled "Present-day Education in Brazil." He completed his doctorate in 1959 and became a tenured professor at the University of Recife's Faculty of Philosophy, Sciences, and Letters. In 1961, the mayor of Recife invited Freire to develop a literacy program for the city that later influenced the creation of the "bare feet can also learn how to read" campaign (ibid).

Freire's literacy programs raised concern and fear from the soon-to-be-established military coup in 1964, which halted all of Freire's work with the poor, illiterate peasants living in northeast Brazil. His literacy program first began in 1962 in the small rural town of Angicos, in Rio Grande do Norte, where some 300 farm workers were taught how to read and write in only 45 days (McLaren, 2000). Freire and his team of cultural workers lived among this group of peasants and workers in order to experience with them the day-to-day realities of their lives. McLaren (ibid) explains Freire's literacy methods succinctly as he describes the role of Freire's cultural or literacy workers as those who were:

> . . . able to help campesinos identify generative words according to their phonetic value, syllabic length, and social meaning and relevance to the workers . . . . Each word was associated with issues related to existential questions about life and the social factors that determined the economic conditions of everyday existence. Themes were generated from these words (words such as "wages" or "government"), which were then codified and decodified by groups of workers and teachers who participated in groups known as "cultural circles" . . . and resulted in a process of ideological struggle and revolutionary praxis—or what was to become famously known as Freirean *conscientização* (p. 143).

Using generative themes to read the word and the world through the process of problem posing, Freire helped peasants and workers gain an awareness, or critical consciousness, or in Freire's words, *conscientizaçâo*. He contextualized the lived experiences of the workers (students) by connecting their social and historical conditions to the larger world around them; he did this through deconstructing words (literacy), so they could understand how their realities were a result of socially constructed policies and ideological agendas that served the interest of those in power. Freire's literacy programs changed the relationship between the traditional role of teacher and student (worker) to one in which the teachers relinquished their authority as the *only* ones who provided knowledge or truth to now acting as facilitators of the learning process. By facilitator, Freire did not mean the role of the teacher was reduced as a mere "guide" who took a backstage seat in the learning process. McLaren (2000) describes the facilitator role as "cobra-like, moving back and forth and striking quickly when the students' conditioning was broken down enough so that alternative views could be presented" (p. 151).

The critical cultural worker acts as the dialectical authority where students are viewed as "subjects" rather than simplified "objects" to be filled with decontextualized, irrelevant information or the drilling of reading and writing skills through technocratic methods. The teacher is a problem poser using students' experiences and knowledge as a means to produce generative themes. Consequently, after generative themes are identified, both teacher and student participate in the process of meaning-making by posing questions, reflecting on and deconstructing them, and finally, reconstructing situations with the goal of inspiring social, economic, and political participation that would improve the standard of living. The end result of this process of politicizing literacy is what Freire refers to as praxis.

As a result of the successful work in Angicos, in 1963, President Joâo Goulart and Minister of Education Paulo de Tarso Santos invited Freire to devise plans to implement 24,000 cultural circles on a national level to address the grim realities of the nation's two million illiterate adult workers (ibid). Unfortunately, in March 1964 all plans came to a halt when a military coup overthrew Goulart's reform-minded administration and suspended all progressive movements. Freire was arrested and imprisoned for 70 days for what was deemed "subversive" activities for his involvement in the national campaign to eliminate adult illiteracy. While imprisoned, Freire was relentlessly interrogated, but his experiences during this time reaffirmed his beliefs and research that education and politics were closely and intricately tied and that in order for change to happen, the masses would have to act; individuals alone could not do it in isolation (Gadotti, 1994, as cited in McLaren, 2000).

Upon his release from prison, Freire sensed his life would be threatened if he remained in his beloved home country. For this reason, he went into a self-imposed exile and sought refuge in Bolivia in September 1964 at the age of 43 (McLaren, 2000). For the next 16 years in exile, Freire travelled the world continuing his fight as a public servant and cultural worker for the poor and oppressed, landing in places such as Chile and Switzerland. He developed literacy programs in various regions including Tanzania and Guinea-Bissau, the former Portuguese colonies of Angola and Mozambique, and São Tomé and Príncipe (ibid.). He worked with the governments of Peru and Nicaragua to revitalize national literacy movements, and in 1969 was appointed a one-year visiting professorship at Harvard University (ibid.). This was a time of social, economic, and political turmoil in the United States, with anti-war protestors objecting to U.S. involvement in Southeast Asia, and university campuses infiltrated with police and militias. Freire realized that even in first-world countries, oppressive conditions suppressed and excluded citizens' rights.

In 1979, Freire was invited back to Brazil. He returned in 1980 and resumed a faculty position at the University of Sao Paulo. He continued his literacy work abroad, aiding numerous countries including Italy, Australia, Angola, and the Fiji Islands (ibid.). From 1989 to 1991, Freire was appointed the municipal secretary of education for the city of São Paulo, where he was responsible for developing literacy reform for two-thirds of the nation's schools.

On May 2, 1997, Paulo Freire passed away as a result of heart failure. Among his influential works read by millions around the world are *Education as a Practice of Freedom*, *Cultural Action for Freedom*, and *Pedagogy of the Oppressed*. Freire's work transcends literacy education and has been studied, read, and included across many scholarly disciplines. Critical scholar and educator Peter McLaren argues that Freire has redefined the meaning of "educator" as one who is viewed as "border intellectual, social activist, critical researcher, moral agent, insurgent Catholic worker, radical philosopher, [and] political revolutionary" (McLaren, 2000, p. 147).

Critical Pedagogy

Freire advocated for liberatory and revolutionary education, one that was transformative and empowering and addressed social and educational injustices. Freire's life work was that of a critical pedagogy in which he challenged hegemony within educational institutions and beyond. He raised questions of inequalities of power that resulted in the oppression or subjugation of culture, education, and language. To this end, "critical theory forms the foundation of critical pedagogy" in an educational sense (Kincheloe, 2004, p. 45). Critical pedagogy examines how these inequalities manifest into everyday educational practices to promote false myths of opportunity and encourage students not to question or challenge the norm. Critical pedagogy rejects complacency and cynicism and instead strives to inspire students to look at "what is" to determine "what could be," and to find a way to move from "where we are" to "where we want to be" (Parmar, 2009, p. 9).

In order to answer these questions, we must be aware of the social, political, and historical factors that contribute to the state of schooling today. Critical educators, as a collective force, identify the structures in place that are preventing more equitable outcomes. As Freire maintained, critical educators cannot move forward without being conscious of the power constructs in place that reproduce such conditions. This is the beginning of social and intellectual emancipation.

A critical pedagogy names the subjects of oppression. Freire deliberately used language that forced individuals to think of the initiator of the action. For example, we often hear the words "disenfranchised" or "at-risk" used within mainstream educational circles. These words are simply coded language that rationalizes deficit theories. When Freire uses the word "oppressed," it begs the questions of who is being oppressed and who is the one oppressing? If there are oppressed people, there must be oppressors. Critical pedagogy refrains from using codified language that neutralizes the problem, or worse, places sole blame on the teacher, student, or family.

Because critical pedagogy names things, we want to name some of the terms we have been using thus far. Who do we mean when we refer to the dominant culture? In the Western world, we are referring to "upper-middle class, white, heterosexual, first language English, and Christian" (Kincheloe, 2008, p. 8). To whom do we refer when we use the terms "oppressed" or "marginalized youth"? This could include many groups, depending on the context in which we are addressing. In schools, we usually refer to those students who are "poor, non-English as first language, gay, lesbian, and bisexual, physically challenged, nonathletic, non-white, overweight, shy, and short" (p. 24). This could also include youth belonging to specific subcultures of youth culture such as hip hop, punk, and goth.

Keeping in sync with naming our subjects, we must name the knowledge that is learned or preferred in schools across America. Influential in the development of critical scholarship is French historian and philosopher Michel Foucault and his notion of power and knowledge. According to Foucault (Rabinow, 1984), we are created by knowledge. But how does knowledge construct our reality? How does it shape our identities? Think for a moment about the knowledge we learn outside of schools. A young child is shaped by the knowledge he or she is exposed to by family members. This in turn shapes the child's identity. When that child grows into adolescence, other forces help construct knowledge and shape identity. These forces are individualized and range from the teen's peer group to the media. If media, for example, plays an influential role in shaping our identities, our views will be limited to what the media presents to us as reality. We could miss out on other kinds of knowledge if we allow only a few sources to construct our reality. Who determines what that reality is? Keeping with the media example, the answer would be those controlling mass communication, or media. If easily influenced or impressionable young people are inundated with media images of expensive materialistic items, such as luxury cars or designer clothing and accessories, the desire to own these products grows stronger and stronger to the point that young people are encouraged to believe that they should own them. In this example, materialistic products become one of the defining factors in shaping identity. We may feel important, beautiful, and entitled if we own such products. We may expect certain treatment if we wear certain clothing brands or drive a luxury vehicle. In a Foucaultian sense, the media, or product, has constructed knowledge and shaped our reality.

But who does this benefit? Those controlling that medium and the corporations behind these products profit by creating another consumer. If mainstream media promotes limited knowledge (e.g., narrow depiction of what is considered beautiful, prescribed gender roles, materialism as a sense of worth and importance), imagine what knowledge they are excluding from mainstream airwaves? We receive limited information because we are so distracted by other "more important" information. We do not participate in this meaning-making process. Instead, it is made for us.

How does education limit or place value on certain knowledge while simultaneously devaluing other knowledge? Traditional and classical education models tend to value the knowledge from those who hold cultural capital. This knowledge is connected to those in the dominant cultural group. When schools validate dominant knowledge or ideologies over subjugated or indigenous knowledge, the result is often marginalization of students from non-dominant cultural groups. When indigenous knowledge or youth literacies are brought into schools as only segments of the school year or part of units of studies in only the social sciences, they tend to remain in the margins resisted by mainstream practices. It is important for educators to be aware of how power and knowledge

Point of Reflection

Can you think of any other examples on how knowledge is constructed for us? Think about your own education: how did it help mold you into the person you are today?

operate in order to counter the perpetuation of such practices. The critical analysis and understanding of culture, knowledge, power, oppression, production, and reproduction of dominant ideologies is an essential component of critical pedagogy. Without this awareness, or what Freire called *conscientização*, students and teachers fail to self-actualize and engage in social and political change.

Critical Literacy: Transforming the ELA Classroom

Teachers engaged in a critical pedagogy are ultimately practicing critical literacy. In our minds, they are one and the same. Once again, we are reminded of Freire's words in the chapter's epigraph, that literacy should no longer be perceived as a skill decontextualized from one's everyday experiences. It is a consciousness of how power constructs dominate in the most subtle, hegemonic ways.

Critical literacy also extends beyond the ELA classroom. This means that English teachers are not the only content-area teachers responsible for teaching literacy. All content-area teachers should be incorporating critical literacy into their classrooms. In doing so, the teacher is inextricably addressing all of the English Language Arts standards of reading, writing, speaking, listening, viewing, and language acquisition, and moving beyond them. Similar to the Writing Across the Curriculum movement, we are promoting a Literacy Across the Curriculum movement, one that is reflective of critical literacy.

Inherent in critical literacy is the need to differentiate instruction because critical educators are aware of the diverse and complex differences their students bring into the classroom. Here again, we emphasize that critical literacy is much more than a teaching strategy; it is an ideology that uses literacy to teach critical thinking to empower students to transform unjust realities.

The term *critical*, though much debated in the field of education (Lankshear, 1997), will be used throughout this text in the original Freirian sense, as a pedagogical tool for the teaching of literacy that exposes and challenges the underlying power structures and inequalities of society. Ultimately, critical educators teach a "reading" of the politics of daily life in hopes that they lead to a "rewriting" of the world in a more democratic fashion (Lankshear & McLaren, 1993). According to Luke, Comber, and O'Brien (1996), "critical literacy requires a 'reading of cultures,' around, behind, underneath, alongside, after, and within the text" (p. 35). Applying a critical-literacy lens to reading sheds light on sociocultural choices, norms, conventions, understandings, and experiences (Browett, 2007). This helps students determine whose social, economic, and political interests are served and why. Uncovering social inequalities and injustices promotes Freire's notion of praxis or agency.

Critical literacy includes cultural and youth texts (or knowledge) alongside the study of the dominant cultural group and critically analyzes all of these texts with rigor. These texts can be introduced in lessons by analyzing written, visual, spoken, auditory, and kinesthetic texts, rather than just that traditional black-and-white print form. Just as Western dominant knowledge is critiqued and challenged for its ideological biases and (mis)representations, critical pedagogues must apply that same rigorous analysis to any marginalized knowledge brought into the curriculum. It is important to include these works because students from historically marginalized or excluded groups feel validated and included when their histories, experiences, and cultures are a central part of the curriculum and not limited to a specialized unit. It is equally important to ensure that students who hold general characteristics of the dominant cultural group do not feel slighted or picked on. The critical teacher must be cognizant that critical literacy is about critiquing how power constructs manifests itself into our everyday lives in effortless, natural, objective ways through policies, practices, beliefs, and attitudes within the educational world and beyond. The critical educator is aware, however, of the powerful hegemonic forces that best serve the dominant culture, and under-represent, misrepresent, or altogether exclude subjugated cultures.

It should be clear by now that critical literacy reaches far beyond acquiring back-to-basics literacies or functional literacy. It includes awareness, understanding, and incorporation of multiple forms of literacy, including but not limited to, computer literacy, emotional literacy, multimedia or multimodal literacies, political literacy, cultural literacy, and media and youth literacies, all in a *critical* manner. The critical educator is aware of the complexities of language as well, and will include these various literacies when appropriate (more on the complexities of language in the form of cultural literacy later). For the student, incorporation of multiple literacies empowers and prepares him or her to meet the ever-evolving changes and demands of society.

Most important, critical educators understand that education is political. This does not mean that teachers exclusively teach the latest political events or have students spit back politicians' names and inauguration dates (though we believe that it is important for students to be aware of what's going in in the political world). Here, we are referring to the awareness that education is inherently political. Education is inherently political when decisions are made about which new teachers to hire, which textbooks or packaged curricular programs are chosen over others, and when

> **Point of Reflection**
>
> Think beyond the English curriculum. How do we teach science, math, history, physical education, art, and music? What decisions were made regarding these curricula? What ideologies are reflected in these decisions?

the English language-arts curriculum requires a certain number of "required" literature to be read, especially when the majority of novels fall under the Western classical canon or literary tradition (Kincheloe, 2004, 2008). Teachers should question the grounds on which these decisions are made. Who made these decisions? Whose interests do these decisions benefit? When U.S. school curricula and practices are grounded in Western histories and dominant ideologies, whose knowledge is centralized and studied?

When you develop your own philosophy of education or pedagogical approach, understand you are creating a political vision. The two are inseparable (ibid). The pedagogical approach required by some school administrators is a political decision. Why "best" practices? What are these "best" practices that are often lauded in mainstream education circles? Who determined they were "best" for your students? The only true expert in knowing "best" practices for your students is you. You work with your students on a daily basis and understand them better than any "best" practices that are forced upon you. The critical teacher knows that what works in the morning may not work after lunch. Or, what works on Monday may not work so well on Friday. As we stated in Chapter One, we do not expect you, alone, to challenge these questions and the people making them. As we warned in the previous chapter, this would be like committing professional suicide. What we ask of you is to connect with like-minded teachers, parents, community organizations, and professors in higher education to resist and change the forces that make your working conditions oppressive and unmanageable.

Think about how literacy is political. As a socially constructed phenomenon, literacy is embedded with the values, beliefs, and ideologies of the group constructing it—the dominant cultural group. Cultural studies and critical theorists argue that membership within the dominant cultural group predisposes its members to social and cultural capital, access to social goods, and power. On the other hand, oppressed groups, like those growing up in an urban low-income neighborhood, predispose their members to social disenfranchisement; these groups carry no special benefits or privileges (Gee, 2008). To maintain these power structures, advantaged groups oftentimes monitor and deny full access to those seeking to join (Delpit, 1995). This can be in the form of educational achievement, language acquisition, and of course, bias. Thus, whether consciously or not, all literacies and the texts they produce are political in nature because they support or challenge social power structures. Youth literacies (explained further in Chapter Three), which tend to be more explicit and carry their political messages closer to the surface, are excellent texts through which teachers can address social inequities, teach students to be critically conscious, and work towards a truly democratic and just society.

Cultural Literacy

As we have explained earlier, teachers must be conscious that "culture" in a critical context is considered in multidimensional ways. Rooted in critical literacy and critical pedagogy is the understanding, awareness, and acceptance of how cultural literacy affects the student–teacher relationship in the classroom. We limit our definition of cultural literacy here and focus in the context of students' language and dialects. In Chapter Three, we expand our definition of culture from a critical perspective and include it in our broader understanding of cultural literacy.

Cultural literacy is understanding, accepting, and validating the language *and* dialects your students bring to the classroom with them. We are referring to language in the form of a second language, specifically addressing your English Language Learners (ELLs), and language in the form of dialects spoken by native English speakers. In the preface to Chapter Four, we provide suggestions and teaching strategies to assist you in understanding and working with your ELLs. We want to focus here on the often ignored discourse of dialectical diversities that you will inevitably encounter when interacting with your students. Consider the following quote from distinguished feminist scholar bell hooks:

> I know that it is not the English language that hurts me, but what the oppressors do with it, how they shape it to become a territory that limits and defines, how they make it a weapon that can shame, humiliate, colonize. (hooks,1994, p. 168)

This quote is hooks' reaction to reading equally distinguished feminist poet Adrienne Rich's poem, "The Burning of Paper Instead of Children." We, too, strongly recommend the inclusion of Rich's poem into your lessons when addressing issues of power, language domination and suppression, and race and class oppression. The above quote is hooks' revelation to one particular line in Rich's poem that reads, "This is the oppressor's language yet I need it to talk to you." This line remained etched in hooks' brain as she was painfully reminded of how close she was to losing her mother tongue, the dialect of Southern Black vernacular speech that she heard and spoke while growing up. She reflected on how her dialect was suppressed while navigating the world of academic writing and within social gatherings. She recalls how editors from academic journals would return her articles transcribed from her dialect to that of Standard (American) English. What message do you think this sends to a person when the dialect s/he grows up hearing and speaking is "corrected"? Realizing that Standard (American) English was a tool that could be used to oppress, dominate, humiliate, and mask speakers of different dialects, hooks resisted the temptation of losing her home dialect. She is reminded of scholar Gloria Anzaldúa's words, "So, if you want to really hurt me, talk badly about my language" (hooks, 1994, p. 168).

Whether we are reflecting on language or dialect, according to the field of sociolinguistics, both are constructed on political, social, and historical contexts—not on science. A person's language and dialect is intricately tied to that person's identity and culture. We must not forget this.

> ### Point of Reflection
>
> When you hear your students speak a different dialect other than the "standard" code, what feelings come to mind? Do you characterize them as "uneducated," speaking "incorrectly," "improper" or as "deficient"? Be honest.

When we work with pre- and in-service teachers, we discuss in depth the variety of dialects that are rooted in just the English language alone. First, we distinguish between Standard English (technically British English, or the Queen's English in sound, syntax, and form) and Standard American English (the standard heard in mainstream news or taught in schools, or written in most U.S. newspapers). We recognize and confirm the diverse dialects that exist in our class, especially Brooklyn vernacular spoken by many of our students, and share perceptions and comments received of it by non-Brooklynites and non–New Yorkers. Our students are made aware that the Standard American English required of them by schools is merely a dialect of the English language that was proclaimed as "standard" by those in power; some scholars often refer to this standard as the "language of power" or "mainstream English." We ask how that particular dialect came to be the "standard." We learn why it is important to navigate between different dialects, or what is known as "code-switching," changing the way we speak depending on the audience we are addressing (Parmar, 2010).

We discuss ways to incorporate home dialects into lessons by providing examples of successful individuals who are from the same dialectical background as their students. Other ways to validate home dialects is to have students create dictionaries that have both their home dialect and the standard code alongside it; role-playing news anchors that tend to speak in Standard American English; translating the meanings of popular musical lyrics, or rap, into the standard code; or writing formal letters, essays, or reports in standard code and creative writing assignments or personal writing journals in their home dialect (Perry & Delpit, 1998). Students who are constantly corrected in written or spoken form for the way they speak or write tend to either resent the teacher for humiliating them in front of their peers; rebel, causing the teacher unnecessary classroom management problems; retreat in silence; rarely participate of their own free will; or worse, succumb to the pressures of speaking "correctly" and lose their home dialect altogether, replacing it with the dominant dialect, or "language of power." As stated above and vehemently again here, we must not forget that language and dialect are both intricately embedded in one's culture and identity. To be clear, what we are arguing here is to teach students how to code-switch in order to successfully navigate through life's complex circles. Our goal as critical educators is that one day, we will not be judged, shamed, humiliated, or oppressed by the way we sound or speak.

Along these lines, our students discuss why codes of convention exist—in this case, Standard American English—and why they must be used, similar to the codes of "professional" dress and "proper" mannerisms that are accepted in certain situations and frowned upon in others. We ask students to reflect on *why* such codes are in effect and *to whom* these codes apply. Why are certain groups relegated to conform to these codes, while others are not? Are people in the dominant cultural group or those in power positions required to use the standard code? How does power or status affect the speech patterns of a person? Are there double standards? Are conditions based on race or class? Do we, as educators, know the difference between dialect and slang? Why is the concept of dialectical diversity a largely uncontested terrain? We ask these same questions to the high school students we have worked with and are enlightened by how much many of them already know about code-switching.

Critical literacy includes dialogue with your students of *why* we must, depending on the audience, learn to speak and write in a dialect different from the student's home dialect. Why are certain language (dominant) ideologies revered and valued and others are not? We hope to dispel myths that to speak in the standard code is talking "educated" or "white," and introduce our students to the political inscriptions of language predicated upon power and ideology. By incorporating the activities and questions above, our aim is to eliminate any association of the standard code to only "white or educated talk" and subsequently the "white is right" axiom we so often hear. Balancing the curriculum to include opportunities to read, see, and hear linguistic and dialectical diversity beyond recognition of only entertainers and athletes is a central component of cultural literacy and critical literacy. We strongly believe all educators, regardless of content and field, should delve deeply into the field of sociolinguistics to learn more about how languages and dialects are constructed purely on political, historical, and subjective means and not on scientific evidence.

As explained in the opening of this section, another element of cultural literacy that we explore is the subcultures of popular and youth cultures. As we maintain in earlier sections, it is important for educators to incorporate the knowledge students bring with them that reflect their culture—or youth culture/youth literacies. In Chapter Three, we explore popular culture, youth culture, and their literacies in depth. If we include popular culture in our lessons, we cannot ignore the influence of mass media on youth. Therefore, we must include a critical examination of mass media and view the various media within it as "texts" that can be critically analyzed.

Critical Media Literacy

The term *critical media literacy* is a part of a critical pedagogy and thus expands upon the notion of critical literacy. Before delving into a description of critical media literacy, we first clarify how literacy is multimodal, creating a pathway to understanding the inclusion of media as texts.

In their work *Multimodal Discourse*, Kress and Van Leeuwen (2001) argue that the monomodal understanding of literacy (literacy as linear and print-based) has largely been replaced with a multimodal understanding of literacy. Multimodality is the "use of several semiotic modes in the design of a semiotic product or event" (Kress & Van Leeuwen, 2001, p. 20). In other words, multimodal texts are embedded with different *modes*: visual, graphic, audio, linguistic, and tactile components that communicate and contribute to the overall understanding of the text (Kress & Jewitt, 2003). Multimodal texts require more than a different set of literacy skills; they require a new definition of literacy and of the reading and writing experiences (Pahl & Rowsell, 2005). There are numerous nonconventional skills used to "read" a single page of multimodal text, for example:

> Take a typical web page. Written parts of the texts are often labels for an image or instructions. Sometimes there are sound bites, there is movement in animated text, there are captions at the bottom related to the text but somewhat outside of it, there are hotspots taking us to another site or another page, there is hypertext giving us definitions, and so on. (Pahl & Rowsell, 2005, p. 35)

Instead of beginning to read from the start of the page, multimodal texts open up the reading experience by giving readers more freedom in how to experience the text (ibid). When reading things online or in different media (like comic books or print and digital advertisements), non-content components like typeface, layout, and graphics play a major role in the reading experience and can either focus or distract the reader from the reading objectives. Over time and through repeated exposure to different multimodal media, users are slowly socialized as to how to approach these types of texts and read them successfully (ibid). Slowly, we are conditioned to read the *manga* (Japanese comics), for example, from right to left and to ignore the extraneous advertisements that appear on the sides of a webpage.

Multimodal texts also have their own conventions, visual design grammar, and as such, different tools for textual analysis. Kress and Van Leeuwen (1996) argue that visual texts have specific types of grammar that can support or challenge the written text. Supporting this idea, Scott McCloud (1993) argues that comic books are structured around frames (the lines around the panels) and gutters (spaces between the lines) that serve as visual closures. When an avant-garde comic artist like Art Spiegelman in *Maus* works outside of these parameters and "bleeds" into these areas, these pages require special critical textual analysis, a different "reading," and serve as a type of visual grammar that adds a nuanced layer of complexity to the overall written plotline. Thus, multimodal texts have different ways of infusing, negotiating, and supporting meaning.

In addition to learning a new way of reading such texts (and arguably all texts, including media as texts), users need to be able to "read" and be aware of the ideologies, messages, and power structures embedded in these types of texts. Because adolescents don't just consume multimodal literacies, but produce them as well, it is essential for them to be aware of the role of the *producer* in texts and to learn to read them with an analytical eye. Pahl and Rowsell (2005) argue that students should learn to see books as "physical live artifacts with a story and a system behind them" (p. 37). This consciousness would not only make adolescents better consumers of multimodal texts, but also make them more aware producers, conscious of the messages, ideologies, and assumptions they are embedding in their multimodal productions. To do this with multimodal texts, students need to be well versed in critical literacy, allowing them to tap into the sometimes hidden motivations of the texts they regularly encounter, including media texts that are highly influential and hegemonic in nature.

Many scholars in cultural studies have defined critical media literacy as the ability to access, decode, analyze, evaluate, and produce communication in a variety of forms, including print and non-print (McLaren, Hammer, Sholle, & Reilly, 1995; Alvermann, Moon, & Hagood, 1999; Potter, 2005). The different forms we are referring to include, but are not limited to, internet, web-based streaming, social media websites, television, film, advertisements, magazines, newspapers, popular music, and radio—we see all of these media as texts. Two of the leading scholars in critical media literacy education, Douglas Kellner and Jeff Share (2009), have pushed for educators to incorporate media education to:

. . . critically analyze relationships between media and audiences, information and power. It involves cultivating skills in analyzing media codes and conventions, abilities to criticize stereotypes, dominant values, and ideologies, and competencies to interpret the multiple meanings and messages generated by media texts. Media literacy helps people to discriminate and evaluate media content, to critically dissect media forms, to investigate media effects and uses, to use media intelligently, and to construct alternative media. (p. 4)

Why incorporate media in your classroom? Besides its being part of popular culture, thus part of youth culture, your students are heavily knowledgeable and influenced by media both positively and negatively. Popular culture, which often addresses and responds to social unfairness and biases, is a powerful site to teach critical media literacy. Morrell (2002) asserts that "popular cultures can help students deconstruct dominant narratives and contend with oppressive practices in hopes of achieving a more egalitarian and inclusive society" (p. 72). Thus, popular culture can be a powerful educational tool that helps us and our students to be critical consumers and producers of media, and also allows us to deconstruct and challenge the power hierarchies of society.

> **Point of Reflection**
>
> Are media texts, to a degree, replacing the teacher or parent in educating children and youth on important issues? If you feel children and youth are highly influenced by mainstream media messages, then why do you think educators aren't incorporating media into their lessons?

Mainstream media is highly influential in constructing reality and shaping students' ideas, beliefs, and values, in essence shaping their identity and perceptions of others different from themselves. This can have potentially devastating effects in terms of perceptions and expectations of others based on race, class, gender, and sexuality. In respect to gender, media is a powerful force in constructing and shaping gender roles, essentially educating children from a very young age of how to behave, which clothing is appropriate, and what toys to play with. Unfortunately, many adults internalize these socially constructed gender roles as well, thereby reinforcing Western dominant ideologies.

When educators engage in critical media literacy, they teach students to identify, reflect on, and challenge the messages, ideologies, and taken-for-granted assumptions embedded in the media they are encountering on a regular basis (Gainer, 2007). Media seen as texts or forms of production provide insight to societal and contextual clues that value dominant cultural attitudes, behaviors, and language while devaluing marginalized or subjugated cultures.

Critical media literacy helps us to identify myths, assumptions, ideologies, power structures, and privilege embedded within the message. Some of these social and contextual clues are often insidious, subliminal, and not always obvious on their surface, resulting in the media-illiterate viewer having very little chance to discover the hidden meanings inherent in media texts. This often results in internalizing messages of "proper" or popular ways to act, dress, speak, and look to be accepted and to be successful.

Critical media literacy is transformative and liberatory in that it creates consciousness as students are able to distinguish between reality and false perceptions. They are engaged in open discussions about mainstream media overrepresentation of particular biases, stereotypes, and dominant viewpoints. Students are taught to deconstruct media messages, stripping away its layers to reveal the power players behind the scenes who are really controlling what we hear, read, and see in media. Questions educators can ask of their students are: Who produces media? Whose interests does the media serve? How does form relate to content? Which codes and conventions are used to cue people on how to respond? How is meaning created? To what extent can people accept media as harmless entertainment, and when should they begin to question media as being unrealistic and problematic? (Kellner, 1995; McLaren et al., 1995; Alvermann et al., 1999; Potter, 2005).

Media-literate students soon discover who the corporate power wielders really are behind television and radio ownership, cable and telecommunications ownership, internet ownership, and print ownership. It suddenly becomes clear that mainstream media in the United States is controlled by a handful of corporations. For example, as of 2011, the U.S. television and radio media landscape has been dominated by (in order of highest to lowest revenue): Comcast Corporation, Walt Disney, News Corporation, Time Warner, Viacom, and CBS Corporation (Freepress, 2009–2012). By examining ownership, annual revenues, and holdings, students determine which corporate conglomerates have merged or acquired other corporations while also understanding the process of a medium's development "from initial production to final production" (ibid.). Equipped with this historical knowledge, students are able to recognize, question, and critically analyze the cultural, social, political, and economic implications of the particular medium studied. This in turn creates not only critically conscious and literate students, but also smart, savvy consumers.

In closing, we remind you that a critical media-literacy program includes examining, interrogating, and analyzing the different forms of media and focusing on reconstructing the meaning of text, and ultimately society. Researching alternative forms of media available on the internet or satellite television serves as a form of including alternative texts, including youth literacies explained in the next chapter. Critical media literacy education requires the teacher allowing access to students' knowledge and expertise in their culture, or youth culture. Given this opportunity, students gain a sense of ownership and become "teachers" of their own histories, experiences, background knowledge, and worldviews. Once these connections are made to the current social structure, schools will help create critically conscious students who are responsible citizens and consumers capable of socially and politically transforming their communities and the larger society.

CHAPTER THREE

The War on Youth Culture

Authentic education is not carried on by "A" for "B" or by "A" about "B," but rather by "A" with "B," mediated by the world—a world which impresses and challenges both parties, giving rise to views or opinions about it. These views, impregnated with anxieties, doubts, hopes, or hopelessness, imply significant themes on the basis of which the program content of education can be built . . . . Many political and educational plans have failed because their authors designed them according to their own personal views of reality, never once taking into account (except as mere objects of their actions) the men-in-a-situation to whom their program was ostensibly directed. (Freire, 1970/2000, pp. 75–76)

This quote by Paulo Freire resonates deeply with many teachers, specifically in regard to the changing demographics of our students and their continued interest in nonacademic forms of literacy. In Chapter One, we explored how the teachers we work with have reported difficulty in meeting standards due to the growing popularity, demand, and use of technology. They report their students are more interested in media or technology-related texts—tweeting, texting, blogging, social networking, maneuvering between iPhones/iPods/iPads, and mastering videogames—than engaging in reading printed materials, especially when reading for pleasure outside of the classroom. Studies have also shown the decline in reading habits among American teens and young adults, which causes grave concerns about educational attainment (NEA, 2007). If educators hope to reach their students and enhance critical literacy, they must learn to respect, acknowledge, and validate the knowledge and experiences their students bring into the classroom, including their interests and expertise from the media-saturated world.

In a 2008 article for the *New York Times*, Motoko Rich explored the future of reading and discovered that the growing popularity of videogames is profoundly reshaping our understanding of literacy (Rich, 2008). The popularity of videogames has made a profound impact on youth, as a recent poll by the Pew Internet & American Life project reports that "97 percent of children 12 to 17 play games on computers, consoles and handheld devices" (Rich, 2008, p. 1). The lines between traditional print-based texts and alternative media texts are blurring as bestselling books like the Harry Potter series and the Inheritance series have developed into web-based online games where gamers can play, chat, and blog on message boards. Packaging videogames and novels as bundles has become popular and has incentivized reluctant readers to not abandon the printed text form. Science-fiction author PJ Haarsma's popular Softwire book series has been packaged with his free online role-playing game, *Ring of the Orbis*, allowing readers of the book series to now actively participate in the story (ibid.). Both printed and digital texts work simultaneously as readers must answer questions from the printed form in order to advance levels in the digital form.

Each year as videogames grow more complex and interactive, players are being given more creative power in the game-playing process and often have the opportunity to produce their own virtual characters, settings, and storylines—a stark contrast from the late 1970s when arcade games entered mainstream society. The interactive and complex nature of videogames today, especially action-oriented or immersion-type games requires the player to act swiftly, while also being analytical. For example, the videogame *Spore* allows players to not only explore, but replicate and actively participate in the evolutionary process. These games seem to be having an effect on brain development. Recent research has found that players of the popular immersion game *Call of Duty: Black Ops* develop more advanced vision, attention, speed, accuracy, and multitasking skills when compared to non-gamers (Trudeau, 2010).

While most adults view videogames with contempt and as cause for academic deterioration, current educational research supports the argument that videogames require and develop specific literacy skills, such as critical thinking, choice-making, understanding semiotics, and plot construction (Gee, 2007). While some researchers argue that videogames can be used as a "gateway drug for [other types of] literacy" (Rich, 2008), others argue that these new media texts shift traditional paradigms about literacy and transform the function of text in the twenty-first-century (Cope & Kalantzis, 2000).

Videogames are only one kind of text that challenges the traditional conceptions and definitions of literacy. Though all texts that are not strictly print-based are generally referred to as "alternative" texts, this chapter will focus specifically on the texts frequented by youth and young adults, texts that involve, create, or explore popular and youth cultures. The disconnect between these types of home/everyday literacies and traditional school-based literacies has been growing steadily wider, leaving students to develop a variety of unique skills outside of school. As reported earlier, despite the fact that 97 percent of adolescents, ages 12 to 17, are engrossed in videogame playing, these digital texts are noticeably absent from mainstream educational discourse. In another example, the explosive popularity of *manga*, Japanese comics, has delighted librarians and publishers around the world, but has failed to catch the attention of educators (Schwartz & Rubinstein-Avila, 2006). Youth writing forums such as those found in teen-created *zines* and weblogs, and youth writing styles such as those used in instant messaging and texting, have an ever-expanding user base, but have failed to significantly alter practice and be fully incorporated in mainstream classrooms (Guzzetti & Gamboa, 2004).

Likewise, the literacy skills being taught in schools are finding little support at home. For example, schools continue to emphasize traditional "back-to-basic" literacy skills while the average American teenager spends 17 hours a week engaging in online activity (Weaver, 2012) and far less time interacting with traditional print-based texts. This presents a major conflict of interests, values, and learning objectives, and can cause school learning to seem irrelevant to adolescent students. Even teachers who are conscious of incorporating new technologies into their classroom instruction often fail to alter their pedagogy in significant ways and simply use advanced equipment to fulfill traditional classroom purposes (Bruce & Hogan, 1998; Cuban, 2003). Perhaps the greatest issue leading this literacy divide is the standards-based, high-stakes testing framework elaborated on in Chapter One, which most schools have been forced to adapt to, causing mandates rather than educational needs and interests to drive instruction (Paugh, Carey, King-Jackson, & Russell, 2007).

Ideally, school is where children should be given the skills with which to navigate, participate, and make sense of the world. Adolescents today interact with a multitude of media in a variety of unique ways. As they respond to online weblogs, play Massively Multiplayer Online Games (MMOG), create YouTube videos, and view advertisements, adolescents are engaging in all different types of literacy practices. These new literacy practices, reflecting

Point of Reflection

If you are a teacher, perform a survey of your high school classroom. Investigate what types of literacies your students invest time in. What types of materials do they read, write, and interact with. Then, share the results with the class and brainstorm ways, with your students, to incorporate more of these materials in your lessons.

Point of Reflection

Reflect on how literacy has evolved since you were in high school. When you were a teenager, what types of literacy did you engage in? Do you think your school adequately prepared you for your future? Think about your students' futures. Brainstorm ways you can include more current forms of literacy to not only engage your students, but better prepare them for their futures.

the new demands of a new age, need to be given more attention by the educational community. Now more than ever, we need to give young people the tools with which to make sense of and "read" this multimedia universe. To do this effectively, educators need to develop a new literacy framework, from our view, framed upon critical pedagogy and critical literacy, that speaks directly to the twenty-first-century literacy experience.

This chapter will explore the literature on pop culture and youth literacies and conclude with ideas of how to incorporate youth literacies into the classroom as a transformative, reflective, and critical experience. We will focus on three topics: (1) how pop culture is defined and interconnected with youth literacies; (2) how teachers view youth literacies and how such texts challenge traditional classroom instruction; and (3) how youth literacies can be used in transformative ways to bridge the home–school literacy divide.

Popular Culture and Youth Literacies

We focus here on the literacy practices of those who are part of youth culture and participate in popular culture. First, we examine what is meant by "youth" to better understand and appreciate all of what youth culture has to offer. The category "youth" has been contentiously debated in academic and public discourses to describe young people in a multitude of ways. From the positivist perspective, using biology as their foundation, children and youth are categorized by age—usually 13- to 25-year-olds—and are viewed as vulnerable, immature, subservient, innocent, and powerless to adult authority (Giroux, 2000; Steinberg, 2011). From this perspective, children and youth are decontextualized, universalized—essentially standardized—objects cruising their way to adulthood. Categorizing youth by age and applying universal rules to their experiences and physical, psychological, and emotional development is merely a tool to justify institutional policies. For this reason, critical researchers argue that experiences of childhood must be understood as social, historical, and political constructions related to power constructs that shape childhood experiences, reducing children and youth to mere entities, and commodifying and oppressing them around the basis of race, class, gender, culture, sexuality, and ability (Giroux, 1996, 2000; Brooks, 2003; Steinberg, 2011). Reducing youth to objects turns them into spectacles or commodities that appeal to consumers of all ages, thus creating an "endorsed and desirable youth market" (Brooks, 2003, p. 2). From this perspective, classifying youth as decontextualized objects has dangerous consequences, resulting in youth culture being regarded as one-dimensional, monolithic, and

Point of Reflection

How do you define pop culture? What experiences or beliefs inform your definition? Do you believe pop culture has a place in the classroom? Why or why not?

pathologizing (Mallan & Pearce, 2003; Steinberg, 2011). In order to understand youth culture better, let's examine pop culture.

Though pop culture is traditionally thought of as cultural activities in which young people invest time in (Duncan-Andrade, 2004), defining pop culture is an arduous task and has been likened to "nailing Jell-O to a wall" (Alvermann & Xu, 2003, p. 146). Part of this difficulty stems from the ever-evolving nature of pop culture and its constant reinvention. Another difficulty is that definitions of pop culture are often based on personal values rather than objective arguments. These "definitions" range from a type of "low culture" (Alvermann & Xu, 2003) that seeks to "socialize people in common ways by exposing them to mindless drivel" (Hagood, 2001, p. 254) to a romanticized "folk culture" that believes "popular culture represents the views of the 'masses'" (Gainer, 2007, p. 108). To define popular culture effectively requires an exploration of one of the most complicated words in the English language: *culture* (Williams, 2006).

Cultural theorist Raymond Williams (2006) offers three working definitions for the term *culture*. First, culture can be defined as "a general process of intellectual, spiritual, and aesthetic development" (p. 90). This means that when speaking of the "cultural development of Western Europe [one would only be referring to] intellectual, spiritual and aesthetic factors—great philosophers, great artists, and great poets" (Storey, 2008, p. 1). This definition of Culture as explained in Chapter Two—intentionally spelled with a capital "C"—places higher value on those groups possessing privilege and living within a particular set of social and linguistic codes. As a result, certain groups possessed cultural capital that the "masses" did not understand, value, or share (Weaver, 2009).

Williams' second definition is that culture refers to "a particular way of life, whether of a people, a period, or a group" (p. 90). Using this broader definition, when speaking of the intellectual, spiritual, and aesthetic development of Western Europe, one would also make sure to include the development of ways of life, for example, the "literacy, holidays, sport, [and] religious festivals [of that particular time]" (Storey, 2008, p. 1).

The last definition Williams suggests is that culture can be used to refer to "the works and practices of intellectual and especially artistic activity" (p. 90). This definition refers to "those texts and practices whose principal function is to signify, to produce, or to be the occasion for the production of meaning" (Storey, 2008, p. 1).

In his book *Cultural Theory and Popular Culture*, Storey argues that Williams' second definition refers to a way of life, a *lived-in* culture, while the third definition refers to signifying practices or texts of meaning-making. Storey suggests that pop culture is ultimately a mobilization of Williams' second and third definitions, a negotiation between creative invention and social practices. Our desire for teachers is to understand the complexities of culture and to view diverse forms of culture as forms of texts and knowledge for inclusion in classroom lesson plans.

Adding to the complexity of pop culture is the term *popular*, which can also be defined in a variety of ways. Storey, citing the work of Williams, offers four conventional uses for the term *popular*: "'well-liked by many people'; 'inferior kinds of work'; 'work deliberately setting out to win favor with the people'; [and] 'culture actually made by the people for the people themselves'" (R. Williams, 1983, p. 237 as cited in Storey, 2008, p. 4). These multiple value-laden definitions of the word *popular* further complicate the issue of defining pop culture because

> . . . any definition of pop culture will bring into play a complex combination of the different meanings of the term 'culture' with the different meanings of the term 'popular'. The history of cultural theory's engagement with popular culture is, therefore, a history of the different ways in which the two terms have been connected by theoretical labour within particular historical and social contexts (Storey, 2008, p. 4).

Therefore, from the cultural studies perspective, popular culture is "in effect an *empty* conceptual category, one which can be filled in a wide variety of conflicting ways, depending on the context of use" (Storey, 2008, p. 1, italics in original).

Working through these difficulties, Storey offers six possible definitions for the term popular culture. First, popular culture can be defined as culture that "is widely favored or well-liked by the people" (p. 4). In other words, popular culture can be defined by a "quantitative index," and determined, for example by, record sales, concert-ticket sales, and box-office earnings, etc. A second definition of popular culture is "left-over 'high culture,'" residual culture that failed to meet the standards of high culture. In this way, popular culture is defined as an inferior culture where "taste," a deeply ideological concept, functions as a class marker. Storey notes the education system supports these class makers by "its promotion of a selective tradition" (p. 6) in the classroom. A third definition defines popular culture as mass culture. From this perspective, popular culture is "hopelessly commercial" (p. 5) and driven by commercialism. Participants of this type of culture are nondiscriminating consumers and mindless customers. A fourth definition of popular culture is as "authentic culture" that originates organically from the people. This highly romantic perspective sees popular culture as folk culture and rejects its commercial elements. A fifth definition of popular culture is based on Antonio Gramsci's concept of hegemony. Countering hegemony in this way, popular culture is a negotiation between the "incorporation of dominant groups" and "resistance by non-dominant groups" (Storey, 2008, p. 8). Suspended between these two tensions, popular culture is a site of ideological struggle, "a terrain marked by resistance and incorporation" (ibid.). The last definition of popular culture, based on postmodernism theory, argues that there is no longer a distinction between "high" and "low" culture and the criteria for determining these distinctions, the set of "high culture" values, has been rejected.

Despite the complexity of popular culture, many educators still view youth culture very simplistically as a passive pastime that corrupts "morals by favourably disposing [young people] towards violence, individualism, hedonism, and materialism" (Kenway & Bullen, 2001, p. 2 as cited in Alvermann & Xu, 2003). Others view popular culture as a one-way act of "mind control" that gives youth the illusion of "false consciousness" (Gainer, 2007). Through exploring the complex nature of culture and its political undertones, Alvermann and Xu propose a new educational framework that recasts popular culture as "everyday culture," where people not only consume, but produce, negotiate, enjoy, and resist images, sounds, symbols, and texts.

The inclusion of popular culture texts, or more specifically, youth literacies, in the literacy curriculum challenges the traditional conception of literacy by supporting the idea that "text is no longer straightforward" (Pahl & Rowsell, 2005, p. 35). For the purpose of this book, we are focusing specifically on one aspect of popular culture: youth culture and its literacies, herein referred to as youth literacies.

From a critical literacy perspective, youth literacies are by definition socially negotiated. Traditionally socially contested spaces, youth literacies are often created in the throes of society and usually respond, criticize, and reinvent conventional understandings. According to Morrell (2002), popular culture "is not an imposed mass culture or a people's culture, it is more than a terrain of exchange between the two" (p. 73), similar to youth literacies. Working from Storey's fifth definition of culture, this view moves popular culture and youth literacies into the "terrain of ideological struggle" (p. 73), a mindful protest expressed through creative uses of music, film, graphic art, and other communicational artifacts familiar to youth. Dynamic in nature, youth literacies are constantly evolving and affecting the spectrum of discourses in which they are situated.

Cultural responsiveness and artistic flexibility tend to make youth literacies excellent political vehicles. While not all youth literacies are explicitly political, Lalik and Oliver (2007) argue that many of these literacies are "intimately related to considerations of issues [including] equity and social justice" (p. 50). According to cultural theorist Andrew Ross (1989), popular culture and youth literacies draw their appeal by rejecting what society considers "educated" taste. In doing this, these texts discard the values of the dominant discourse and push for a more pluralistic perspective that more accurately represents the spectrum of social tastes and ideals.

Teachers' Views of Youth Literacies & Instructional Challenges

Among adults, teachers could potentially have the most exposure to youth literacies. Yet unfortunately, most fail to utilize the opportunities their close proximity affords them and do not view these literacies as "school-worthy" (Duncan-Andrade, 2004). In fact, most teachers view such texts as deviant and antithetical to academic goals (ibid.). By taking this position, teachers shut a valuable window into their students' literacy practices, interests, and meaning-making processes (Alvermann & Hagood, 2000). A reconceptualization of popular culture texts as rich valued youth literacies would give teachers an avenue through which to explore alternative perspectives and enrich the traditional canon. This shift in perspective would reframe youth culture to be used by teachers to develop and enhance literacy instruction.

Although there are teachers who do value youth literacies and use them in the classroom, many often fail to use these texts in transformative ways (Morrell, 2002). Duncan-Andrade argues that teachers tend to use youth literacies in the classroom as a reward after students have completed working on more "important" academic work (2004). Most commonly, this takes the form of a film after a unit of study has been completed. Using youth literacies in this way sends a number of messages to students. First, because it is not viewed as a text, the film is not seen as something worthy of intellectual interrogation. Second, students are not taught to see their "engagement with media as a form of literacy development" (Duncan-Andrade, 2004, p. 322). Finally, students are not given the skills through which to analyze and critique their own media interactions. In a research study, Morrell found that even teachers who desire to use youth literacies in critical ways often fail to do so. Part of this failure is because students have not "owned" this type of thinking and are simply parroting back what they think the teacher wants to hear.

This problem also results from a teacher-centered, positivist pedagogical model and a failure to realize that transformative teaching requires a shift in pedagogical design. According to critical scholar Lawrence Grossberg (1994), there are four major pedagogical frameworks that are commonly practiced. The first and most conventional framework is what Grossberg refers to as hierarchical practice. In this model, the classroom is teacher-centered and the teacher is the "judge and jury of truth" (Duncan-Andrade, 2004, p. 314). This model is similar to Friere's criticism of the banking model (1970/2000). In this model, students are viewed as incompetent, devoid of experiences and personal knowledge; essentially, students are seen as empty vessels waiting to be "filled" with the knowledge of the teacher.

Grossberg's second framework, called dialogic practice, attempts "to avoid a teacher-centered system of knowledge control by creating opportunities for the silenced to speak for themselves" (Duncan-Andrade, 2004, p. 315). In this system, teachers operate out of critical awareness and attempt to remedy social injustices and power inequalities by setting up opportunities for the "voiceless" (minority and marginalized students) to speak. The potential problem with this approach, as Grossberg points out, is that the teacher may incorrectly assume that these "voiceless" students have not yet set up their own sophisticated forms of communication. These students have their own (cultural) literacies in their own language and dialects, literacies that the teacher is unaware of or invalidates because they are not legitimized or validated by the institution of school.

The third framework, praxical pedagogy, creates a transformative learning environment in which students are given the tools to "intervene in their own history" (Grossberg, 1994, p.16). Here we must be mindful to avoid operating "from the deficit perspective" (Duncan-Andrade, 2004, p. 315) that fails to see our students as competent in affecting their own transformation. Teachers must also be aware that by insisting on having the "answer" and claiming to possess the special "formula" for the students' transformation, they are assuming that students have not already been involved in their own transformation (Frechette, 2002). Essentially, though unintentionally, being unaware of these dynamics would replicate the very oppressive conditions teachers are seeking to transform (Grossberg, 1994; Duncan-Andrade, 2004; Hyland, 2005; Gainer, 2007).

It is in Grossberg's fourth framework, the pedagogy of articulation and risk (1994), that educators relinquish absolute educational authority, but do not deny all claims to authority (Frechette, 2002). As explained in Chapter Two, this means that teachers acknowledge their role in the school institution and examine their own position within and in relation to the power structures of society (Grossberg, 1994; Frechette, 2002). Developing a pedagogy of articulation and risk also requires educators to take "risks" in their own thinking and move beyond the safety zones of instruction. To do this effectively, teachers must acknowledge that they do not have all the answers, and they must be aware of the complexity of culture and their students' rich lives both inside and outside of school. Ideally, teachers of "risk and articulation" do not even know exactly where their lessons will lead, but embark on an authentic learning journey with their students.

A pedagogy of articulation and risk also gives students the space to derive pleasure and critique their favorite texts simultaneously. This includes the inclusion of popular culture, youth literacies, and media texts critiqued from a critical media literacy lens. As Gainer (2007) points out, "critical media literacy is sometimes seen as being at odds with children's pleasure, even leading children to 'lie' by criticizing mainstream media in order to please the teacher" (p. 112). Oftentimes, teachers fail to realize that engaging in critical analysis does not necessarily "have to involve taking a negative stance, rather it includes looking at an issue or a topic in different ways, analyzing it and hopefully being able to suggest possibilities for change" (Vasquez, 2005, p. 205 as cited in Gainer, 2007). For example, while observing his daughter dancing to what he considered a misogynistic song, Gainer noted that his daughter was able to both derive pleasure while critiquing its message. Alvermann, Moon, and Hagood (1999) support this argument, stating that critical analysis and pleasure need not be at odds with each other. Indeed, when working with these forms of texts, they caution teachers to do so thoughtfully and avoid a "liberating" stance that prevents students from vocalizing their enjoyment of such materials.

> ## Point of Reflection
>
> What kind of pedagogical framework do you employ? Why? Is this your ideal? How do you envision your classroom operating? What steps can you take today to mobilize your vision?

Bridging the Home–School Literacy Divide

Today more than ever before, young people are immersed in literacy (Williams, 2008). With the creation of Twitter, Facebook, and YouTube, society is moving further and further away from a traditional conceptualization of literacy to a time when "life on the screen is an everyday, natural practice—[and adolescents] know no other way of being" (Kress, 1997, p. 167). Undoubtedly, we are living at a time when "literacy practices are being fundamentally altered" (Williams, 2008, p. 682) and taking a new direction. These shifts must be acknowledged, and educators need to re-examine the role of literacy instruction in the twenty-first century. Without this reflection, these two different literacy directions create a divide that fails young people on two accounts: (1) it makes traditional texts seem irrelevant and out of touch with the modern life, and (2) it fails to teach good critical media analysis with which to navigate the multimedia literacies. In addition, this divide creates a situation of competing literacy interests, with each approach vying for the attention of adolescents. Eventually, most researchers agree that traditional school-based literacies will lose this battle because:

> With the growing pervasiveness and persuasiveness of twenty-first-century youth culture, most particularly the media (television, music, videogames, movies, and magazines), traditional school curriculum, coupled with traditional pedagogies, stand little chance for capturing the hearts and minds of young people (Duncan-Andrade, 2004, p. 317).

Many researchers argue that instead of working in opposition, youth literacies and school-based literacies must be re-envisioned into one cohesive set of literacy objectives (Alvermann & Xu, 2003; Gainer, 2007; West, 2008; Williams, 2008). Though this in itself requires a major discussion, youth literacies as texts can easily be used across the curriculum and are especially compatible with the English Language Arts. These texts can be used in a number of transformative ways, even when working within a standards-based framework (Paugh et al., 2007). Youth literacies can be used to make home–school connections and validate "students' diverse cultural and linguistic experiences both in and out of school" (Alvermann & Xu, 2003, p. 157). For example, watching an episode of *Dora the Explorer*, which features a bilingual young girl, can teach English Language Learners to appreciate and celebrate their own linguistic diversity (Alvermann & Xu, 2003). Youth literacies are also wonderful ways to teach reading and other language arts concepts along with critical media literacy. For example, students can make text-to-world connections by discussing feminism through an analysis of the gender biases and stereotyping of female superheroes in comic books. Students can also compare and contrast texts and films, for example "the portrayal of heroes in Western epics with . . . [Francis Ford] Coppola's Michael Corleone" in the Godfather trilogy (Morrell, 2002, p. 75). In writing, teachers can create online literary-response blogs (West, 2008) and stop viewing the presence of computer-mediated communication (CMC) such as instant-messaging in formal writing as "mistakes" (Jacobs, 2008). Instead, teachers can begin to view such "miscues" as opportunities to "raise students' metacognitive awareness of their writing skills . . . as well as decision-making process" (Jacobs, 2008, p. 209).

These are just some of the numerous ways teachers can tap into the multiple youth literacies that young people are invested in. As you create your next lesson plan, consider that 53 million Americans, many of whom are youth, are digital content creators

Point of Reflection

What needs to change about the curriculum to account for technological advancements? What changes must be made to teaching now that it is easier to access primary sources? How should we rethink ideas of literacy when students are asked to not only be readers but writers, editors, collaborators, contributors, and publishers? How can learners take advantage of the opportunities such tools present?

(Richardson, 2008). Think of what it means to be an educator of this unparalleled generation. Experiment with the powerful and oftentimes free technologies that are available. Join an online educational community for support and ideas, create a class wiki, form a book-club blog, or create a class radio station. While these changes undoubtedly present a challenge to educators, it is also an extremely exciting time in the field. As you balance test preparation and learning standards, we encourage you to nurture your own sense of wonderment and foster your own creativity as to what these powerful new kinds of texts can accomplish.

Using youth literacies in this unconventional way not only teaches students traditional literacy concepts, but does so in a relevant and engaging way, using critical media literacy as its foundation. Because "pop culture texts are a part of students' everyday literacies, they hold powerful and personal meanings for students" (Alvermann & Xu, 2003, p. 158). Teachers should tap into these powerhouse texts and use them in transformative ways. Not only would this engage students in learning, but it would make education a more relevant, reflective, critical, transformative, and eventually, a more truly democratic institution.

Where Do We Go from Here?

As should be clear by now, and further substantiated by a report by Education Sector, the current "back-to-basics" literacy approach is not adequately preparing students for the twenty-first-century world (Silva, 2008). While "basic skills are necessary, they are not sufficient" (Silva, 2008, p. 2) and do not speak directly to the modern literacy experience. While the Common Core State Standards are intended to make up some of these gaps they have yet to be field tested in schools, therefore it is not yet known how they impact student learning. Across the spectrum, the traditional conception of literacy is being challenged and revised. International organizations such as National Research Council, Organisation for Economic and Co-operative Development, and the International Society for Technology in Education agree that complex thinking and analytical skills are an integral part of learning at every stage of development (Bransford, Brown, & Cocking, 2000) and must be incorporated in the classroom at every level.

Though the world has dramatically changed in the past few years, schools have failed to truly acknowledge and respond to these new realities. Educators must revisit the underlying assumptions of current educational practices and question whether these objectives truly meet the needs of today's twenty-first-century students. We encourage teachers to start acknowledging these changes by incorporating youth literacies in the classroom framed by

Point of Reflection

If you are a teacher, revisit one of your instructional units and look for ways to incorporate youth literacies. If you've never designed a unit, think about ways you can incorporate youth literacies in the future. Share with a colleague (or even your students) your goal to include some aspect of youth literacies. Together, brainstorm ways to meet this objective. Conduct an informal assessment to evaluate how your students met (or will meet) the objectives of the unit. Share your findings with a supervisor or with your colleagues.

critical literacy and critical media literacy. Such practices would not only engage students, but bridge home and school literacy practices, and ultimately encourage the acquisition of skills in a manner that is contexualized and *critical*, which is necessary in order to be successful in the twenty-first century.

Teachers need to reflect on their own understanding of youth culture and the literacies within it. After careful research, teachers should work at incorporating these literacies in their classroom and making them a fundamental part of the curriculum. Such action would transform the classroom in a variety of ways. First, it would engage students and help them see school as a relevant part of their lives. Second, it would develop critically literate students equipped to function successfully in the modern world. Finally, it would create a more balanced and democratic curriculum and give students opportunities to be agents of social and political change.

Incorporating youth literacies in the classroom has potential to also affect policy in a variety of ways. First and foremost, it would challenge the way literacy is viewed at the local, state, and national levels, and force officials to redefine literacy and identify the skills that are truly needed to be successful in the twenty-first century. This would ultimately lead to a new framework of assessment, one that is more open ended and develops complex, analytical, and creative thinking. Second, using youth literacies as part of the official school program would require a re-examination of culture and what is generally accepted as "curriculum." Finally, teaching youth literacies with a more reflective, critical pedagogy would make education an open-ended, exploratory, learning process, a truly democratic and transformative experience rather than the forced acquisition of the dominant discourse.

As we have stated in previous chapters, this book serves as a guide—or gentle push—for teachers to supplement their standardized curriculum from the perspective of critical pedagogy using critical literacy. Our goal is not to create another prepackaged, standardized literacy program for teachers to passively integrate into their curriculum. Instead, we provide pedagogical suggestions and critical questions and activities that teachers can take (or not) and adapt to their own unique classroom dynamics. In Chapters Four through Seven, we provide sample unit plans of four classical and four "alternative" novels that apply critical literacy questions and activities.

Point of Reflection

Imagine being freed from the world of standardized testing, stressful supervisors, and pay cuts. What is your vision of twenty-first-century education? Either free write, draw, or simply think about how we will educate kids in the future. Will there be buildings? Desks? Books? What will your curriculum look like? What forms of technology will you incorporate? Given our expanded definitions of "text" and "culture," what forms of text and culture will you include in your teaching? What—and whose—knowledge will you include? Share your vision with a colleague and discuss its current implications.

A Guide to Using the Unit Plans in Chapters Four through Seven

These unit plans are designed to introduce you to teaching critical literacy as described in Chapter Two. They are also meant to invigorate your existing curriculum by encouraging you to try alternative teaching styles, include creative activities, and tackle challenging topics. Additionally, by interweaving traditional and alternative school texts, many of these unit plans are easily adaptable and will simply build on your existing curriculum.

The General Framework

The unit plans are divided into chapters. Each chapter is a self-contained unit centering on two primary texts: one classic school reading and one alternative text. Though reading is the primary avenue of exploration, each unit is embedded with a variety of different literacy activities including creative writing, journalism, photography, art, and music.

Each unit is designed for class use. This framework includes an introduction to the unit, guidelines for how to use the unit, and a general outline. Each text is accompanied by a brief summary, a pre-reading activity, discussion topics, review questions, learning activities, and a post-reading activity. Each unit also contains numerous ideas on how to take the lessons a step further to expand on the activities and differentiate instruction. Many activities are accompanied by a printable guide found in the Appendix. Although critical literacy questions and activities are infused throughout each unit, please refer to the "Critical Literacy/ Critical Textual Analysis" guide found at the end of the Appendix

to apply additional questions to each unit of study (or any literature you teach).

Differentiating Instruction: Content, Process, and Product

Keep in mind that critical literacy questions and activities are designed to differentiate instruction in multiple ways: by content,
process, and product.

The *content* of each unit comprises questions that range from
low-order to high-order critical-thinking skills based on Bloom's
Taxonomy. Bloom's Taxonomy–type questions are not reflective
of critical literacy, but we feel they hold *some* weight in the process
of reading and comprehending any text. There is no need to create
more than one lesson plan. Differentiation is evident in critical literacy questions and activities that are contextualized and relevant
to students' lives, interests, and knowledge base. Critical literacy
uses a scaffolding approach, or as Freire argued, the incorporation
of generative themes to read the word and the world through the
process of problem posing. We teach by breaking down or deconstructing the "whole" (world) into smaller "parts" (word) only to
build back to, or reconstruct, the "whole" (world). In the process,
students participate in the educational experience by including
their knowledge and experiences in the curriculum content while
engaging in authentic conversations and activities that require
critical complex understanding of the theme under investigation.
The teacher and students use generative themes to construct questions and activities that promote agency (activism). We have provided some of these questions and activities for you based on our
working with—and learning from—other teachers and students.

The *process* of differentiation is evident in critical pedagogy
when incorporating multiple strategies into your lessons. A critical pedagogue understands students learn differently and at different paces. To this end, we strongly encourage you to get to know
your students and understand their strengths and weaknesses in
terms of their ability level. We encourage you to use the questions and activities provided in the following chapters as a guide
to accomplish this in creative ways. At times, students will work
individually, in small groups, or with a partner. Depending on the
activity, students may be placed heterogeneously (mixed-ability
level) or homogeneously (same-ability level). A discussion may be
in the form of debate in which the class is split into two large
groups, or even one large group involving the entire class.

When differentiating instruction, we encourage teachers to
consider Howard Gardner's "Theory of Multiple Intelligences"
(Smith, 2008) and to incorporate as many of his intelligences as
possible. We make specific use of Gardner's linguistic intelligence

in activities that explore the cultural and dialectical diversity of our students. We also embedded many opportunities for students who have strong interpersonal and intrapersonal intelligences by posing thought-provoking questions to initiate authentic conversations. Interpersonal intelligence requires critical reflection and understanding of moods, desires, and motivation. In other words, how do people operate? And what motivates them to act in certain ways? Intrapersonal intelligence requires critical reflection of "self," including how beliefs and ideological positions are formed. Understanding how "self" operates means understanding one's feelings, desires, strengths, and weaknesses, and how these components will guide behavior. We also include activities that incorporate visual and auditory strengths when we use graphic organizers, art, photography, graphic novels, technology, or when we have students analyze or listen to videos, media texts, and music. Students strong in bodily-kinesthetic abilities are given opportunities to express their work by engaging in activities in their communities and through the performance arts: theatre, role-playing, spoken word, rap, or dance.

The *product* of differentiation is the use of multiple assessment measures to monitor student progress. A critical pedagogue encourages performance- and project-based assessment tools. As described in Chapter Two, the student–teacher relationship changes to one in which the teacher is seen as a facilitator, with authority. This provides opportunities for students to teach the teacher by incorporating their knowledge and opinions into the curriculum. This balanced approach to learning where both students and teachers learn with—and from—each other allows for assessment to be ongoing and interactive.

Reaching Everybody: Ideas for English Language Learners (ELLS)

In respect to *content*, the questions provided in each unit reflect awareness and understanding of cultural and ethnic diversity. Incorporating, appreciating, and celebrating cultural diversity is an important element in differentiating instruction to meet the needs of both English Language Learners (ELLs) and non-ELLs. The units we include in the following chapters incorporate interactive activities, small-group work, thematic units, and integrated learning experiences, all of which serve to enhance learning opportunities for ELLs. ELLs enter your classroom with rich, complex cultures, histories, and experiences. To gain valuable insight into their worlds, we recommend that you ask your ELLs if they are comfortable sharing their personal stories with the rest of the class. Although many of the *activities* suggested in each unit were written with ELLs in mind, we have included a few activities that specifically target the needs of ELLs. These activities are also beneficial for non-ELLs and will be designated by the following symbol:

The *process* and *product* of differentiating instruction for ELLs are broad and varied. There is a tremendous amount of research available that prepares teachers in understanding and appreciating working with ELLs. We offer few strategies below.

Grouping: Pair proficient or fluent ELLs with less proficient ELLs. Or pair proficient ELLs with English-speaking students. Another option, if possible, is to pair ELLs with older, more proficient ELLs.

Processing: It is important to remember that ELLs need time to process questions and/or instructions. Do not be impatient if the student does not respond quickly. Similarly, the teacher should be aware of his/her speaking pace and pause often to allow ELLs time to process. Also, avoid common "American" idioms that may be foreign to the ELL. Idioms such as "it's raining cats and dogs," "cat got your tongue?" "money talks," "play it by ear," or "take the bull by its horns" (and many others) may confuse ELLs who may take these statements quite literally. If you use popular idioms, make sure to explain the meaning. Restate complex sentences without dumbing down the original intent of the sentence. Sequence a series of simple sentences when restating a complex sentence.

Questioning: Ask open-ended and high-order thinking questions that require thoughtful responses. Do not dumb down instruction. Ask students to compare and contrast, explain, describe, or draw conclusions. This requires the ELL to practice using the second language.

Code-switching: Do not penalize ELLs if they insert words or short phrases from their native tongue while answering partly in English. Because they need time to process information, some ELLs will resort to this form of code-switching in which both languages are infused while responding. An example may be, "*Aye dios mios!* I forgot my lunch today!" or "We have to ask *papi* permission to go to the party."

Celebrating Mistakes: When working with ELLs, it is important to remember that errors are indicators of learning. When the goal is to have ELLs engage in sustained dialogue or discussions, try not to correct specific errors that are made by the ELL. Rather, allow the ELL to continue the dialogue and when appropriate, the teacher can restate what the ELL said to model correct form. Understand too, that errors can indicate progress as the ELL is making an effort in processing the language. While we understand that correcting is necessary, we urge you to use common sense in the timing of your corrections. Research has found that frequent corrections discourage participation and hinders ELLs' efforts in expressing thoughts and opinions, resulting in silencing of the student.

Understanding Native Languages: If possible, familiarize yourself with the grammatical rules and/or native language of your ELLs. By doing this, you will better understand the process that ELLs take when decoding and constructing the second language (English). Grammatical rules and patterns vary by language system. ELLs often apply the rules in their home language when constructing sentences in the second language. For example, it is common for native Spanish speakers to omit the subject in the sentence, whereas in English, the subject is always necessary. Along these lines, do not assume the ELL is proficient in his/her native language. Just because we hear the ELL speaking in his/her native language, we cannot assume s/he is *academically* proficient.

Respecting Process: Set high expectations for ELLs. Realize that learning a second language is a difficult and long process that typically takes five to seven years to acquire *academic* proficiency. Respect the language and culture of your ELLs.

Structuring Class: Create predictable, instructional routines for ELLs. All students benefit from structured environments, even in the critical pedagogue's classroom. Are there specific times to hand in homework? Is there a designated space to place homework, hall passes, or personal belongings in the classroom? Structured environments and practicing regular routines helps ELLs concentrate their time, focus, and energy on instruction and content.

Meaning-making: ELLs, like most of us, are visual learners. Provide visual images when possible so ELLs can associate words with pictures. Use technology to show images. When possible, have ELLs and non-ELLS work together and act out or role-play words, expressions, or short messages. Use visual organizers and graphics to point out key concepts or themes.

Modeling: Model the English language for ELLs. Implement read-alouds and think-alouds so ELLs can hear the language being spoken and copy the process of thinking about a text.

Incorporating Texts: Use bilingual dictionaries, translators, or technology if available. Provide handouts to ELLs in advance. Hang bilingual signs around the room for both your ELLs and non-ELLs to learn from. Along these lines, hang diverse cultural posters on the walls that represent the ELLs' backgrounds.

Networking: Seek other resources. Reach out to other teachers and students in your school who are proficient in the second language of your ELL. This includes the ELLs' family and community members. Invite speakers to your class to not only help you and your ELL, but to act as a guest speaker sharing stories and experiences of the culture in which the language is situated. This fosters a sense of community and celebration of diversity within your class.

Using Literature to Explore Class, Race, Gender, and Power

While these units are intended to develop critical literacy in your classroom, each unit centers on a specific topic and theme. In the fourth chapter, *Lord of the Flies* and *Push* are the primary texts used to explore issues of class. The fifth chapter centers on *A Step from Heaven* and *The Absolutely True Diary of a Part-time Indian* and focuses on the subject of race. The sixth chapter includes *The House on Mango Street* and *Persepolis* and aims to unravel the politics of gender. In the final chapter, *Fahrenheit 451* and *Maus* are used to expound on broad issues related to the uses and abuses of governmental power. We recognize that all the themes of class, race, gender, and power can be found in all eight texts and strongly encourage teachers to address them whenever possible.

It is important to recognize that these lesson plans are not only designed with content that encourages critical literacy, but to deliver that material in a manner that encourages this kind of pedagogy as well. For this reason, activities are largely collaborative in nature. Staying true to a critical pedagogy, the teacher plays the role of "facilitator," thereby keeping lectures to a minimum; students are encouraged to explore and interact with the materials, achieving learning through personal reflection, authentic conversation, and engaging in critical thinking activities that will result in social and political awareness and agency. Here, reading skills, which are so often the sole focus of language-arts classes, are not occupying center stage, but serving as a scaffold, a means by which students arrive at the real purpose of learning: comprehension and retention of meaningful, relevant knowledge that propels students to participate as active agents of change in their communities and the larger society.

Meeting National Standards

Though the subject matter may seem radical, these lesson plans meet all of the learning standards set forth by the National Council of Teachers of English (NCTE) and the International Reading Association (IRA). Here, we intentionally include the NCTE/IRA Standards over the Common Core State Standards (CCSS) because at time of publication, the CCSS have yet to be fully implemented or tested in schools. Additionally, both NCTE and IRA are long-standing organizations comprised of English education and literacy professionals. We hope this emphasizes that it is possible to meet all learning standards without standardizing learning.

1. Students read a wide range of print and nonprint texts to build an understanding of texts, of themselves, and of the cultures of the United States and the world; to acquire new information; to respond to the needs and demands of society and the workplace; and for personal fulfillment. Among these texts are fiction and nonfiction, classic and contemporary works.

2. Students read a wide range of literature from many periods in many genres to build an understanding of the many dimensions (e.g., philosophical, ethical, aesthetic) of human experience.

3. Students apply a wide range of strategies to comprehend, interpret, evaluate, and appreciate texts. They draw on their prior experience, their interactions with other readers and writers, their knowledge of word meaning and of other texts, their word identification strategies, and their understanding of textual features (e.g., sound-letter correspondence, sentence structure, context, graphics).

4. Students adjust their use of spoken, written, and visual language (e.g., conventions, style, vocabulary) to communicate effectively with a variety of audiences and for different purposes.

5. Students employ a wide range of strategies as they write and use different writing process elements appropriately to communicate with different audiences for a variety of purposes.

6. Students apply knowledge of language structure, language conventions (e.g., spelling and punctuation), media techniques, figurative language, and genre to create, critique, and discuss print and nonprint texts.

7. Students conduct research on issues and interests by generating ideas and questions, and by posing problems. They gather, evaluate, and synthesize data from a variety of sources (e.g., print and nonprint texts, artifacts, people) to communicate their discoveries in ways that suit their purpose and audience.

8. Students use a variety of technological and information resources (e.g., libraries, databases, computer networks, video) to gather and synthesize information and to create and communicate knowledge.

9. Students develop an understanding of and respect for diversity in language use, patterns, and dialects across cultures, ethnic groups, geographic regions, and social roles.

10. Students whose first language is not English make use of their first language to develop competency in the English language arts and to develop understanding of content across the curriculum.

11. Students participate as knowledgeable, reflective, creative, and critical members of a variety of literacy communities.

12. Students use spoken, written, and visual language to accomplish their own purposes (e.g., for learning, enjoyment, persuasion, and the exchange of information).

CHAPTER FOUR

Class Wars

Lord of the Flies Meets Precious

"Open your notebook, Precious."
"I'm tired," I says.
She says, "I know you are but you can't stop now, Precious, you gotta push."
And I do.
                    —Precious Jones in *Push*, (Sapphire, 1996, pp. 96–97)

As educators we are politicians; we engage in politics when we educate. And if we dream about democracy, let us fight, day and night, for a school in which we talk to and with the learners so that, hearing them, we can be heard as well. (Freire, 1998, p. 68)

Why Talk about Class?

Blue collar, white collar, pink collar, white crust, dirt-poor, middle class, working middle class—social labels are as broad and as complicated as the economic spectrum. These labels are not value free. In fact, most researchers believe that social class plays a powerful role in learning development; some even argue that social class impacts school performance more than involved parenting (Shepherd, 2010). From a critical-literacy perspective, social class is an unavoidable reality. Students arrive to school each day with and within their individual life stories and histories, stories that can be debilitating and disempowering. Despite this truth, most teachers pride themselves in treating all students equally, unwilling and/or unable to address their very important differences and needs.

Critical educators believe that the key to tolerance lies in acknowledging and rectifying issues of class. This process is fueled by critical consciousness. This kind of awareness is proactive and can be fostered by acknowledging the different realties and experiences within the classroom. To encourage students to develop critical consciousness, educators should engage their students in authentic dialogue.

In our experience, this conversation is best initiated by sharing your own personal experiences with class, thereby creating a safe, patient, and welcoming environment for your students to follow suit. But this is often not enough. For many, there is no metaphor, no working language or vocabulary with which to discuss these complex issues. This is where great literature steps in. Stories provide a powerful lens with which to explore issues of class.

Lord of the Flies and *Push* are two such stories, both being very different representations of the fluidity and permanence of social structures. In *Lord of the Flies*, (Golding, 1959/2011) a classic high school text, a group of school boys is marooned on a deserted island. There, they create a destructive, dysfunctional, and violent social system with murderous leaders, naïve followers, and social outcasts. In *Push* (Sapphire, 1996), a very unconventional high school text, Precious is the illiterate product of her welfare-dependent life. Through literacy, she learns to resist the life set for her, choosing instead to become an empowered voice of the future.

How Do I Use This Unit?

This unit offers two very different perspectives on social order. *Lord of the Flies* is told in the third person, giving the reader a bird's-eye view of the narrative, which allows for easy analysis on how class systems are formed and maintained. In contrast, *Push* is told in the first person, offering the reader an intimate view into Precious' journey as she *pushes* against her social circumstances. Both of these narratives can serve as lenses, historical and contemporary, and provide a window into another time and world. Though not the main focus of this unit, these texts also illuminate some interesting gender differences as *Lord of the Flies* centers on a group of young men, while *Push* focuses on the struggle of a young woman. Additionally, both of these narratives offer incisive racial commentaries as *Lord of the Flies* documents the adventure of a group of white, privileged Anglo boys, while *Push* centers on escaping the brutalities of the African American experience.

This unit is divided into several parts. These parts are intended to be phases, steps that move inwardly and become more reflective in nature. The accompanying activities are also designed to provide a mirror to you and your students' own lives. To this end, the literature is used as a tool for analysis, helping learners acquire the language with which to talk about these issues.

Word of warning, while *Lord of the Flies* is popular high school reading, *Push* is not. It may be difficult to get permission to read this text with your students. From our experience, there are a number of ways to overcome this dilemma. First, with proper permission, copy large excerpts from the text and black out words that your school does not approve of. Second, simply recommend the book to your students and ask them to read it outside of class because it is too "controversial" to read in school (you'll be surprised how many students will read it!). Third, appeal to parents directly with a permission slip. Finally, as a last resort, watch the movie with your class and discuss the themes afterwards.

Text 1: *Lord of the Flies* by William Golding (1959)

Lord of the Flies is one of the most popular books read in high schools across America. In many ways it is the quintessential classic: a British boys' adventure story expertly written with compelling messages about impulse control, power, adolescence, and violence. Though it is traditionally constructed, *Lord of the Flies* is loaded with rich complexities and subtle nuances. Its study of power, violence, and class lends itself beautifully to a critical-literacy interpretation.

> ### What Is *Lord of the Flies* About?
> *Lord of the Flies* opens with a group of British school boys recently marooned on an uninhabited tropical island. Initially the boys mimic their own civilization and try to establish a democracy. After a bitter struggle for power, the democracy unravels. The majority of the boys turn to a life of totalitarianism and savagery, shedding all sense of morality, eventually killing one another.

Lesson Opener: Policy Debate

This activity can work well in an election year. In the event that there are no national, state, or local elections, or if time is limited, host a small-scale election in which the candidates argue for class policy changes (recess rights, student government, homework rules, etc.).

Elect two students from the class to be candidates. These students must run for election and convince as many students in the class to vote for them. After giving the candidates some time to prepare, host a debate during which students have an opportunity to question the candidates' positions on key issues. Explain to the candidates that in order to be named the winner, they must win the majority of their classmates' votes. They must do everything within their legal power to guarantee as many votes possible. After the debate, have each student cast a ballot in privacy, after which the ballots should be counted and the winner announced.

Though this activity will no doubt be fun for some students, it is the discussion after the election has concluded that is most enlightening. This brief activity is an introduction to how power dynamics work. In this mock election, one person tries their hardest to secure as much power possible to achieve a desired goal. To make students aware of these nuances, explore the following questions:

For the voting students:

- What convinced you to vote for your candidate?

- Did your commitment to one candidate ever waiver? How did you resolve your doubt?

- Are you pleased with the election's results? Why or why not?

For the candidates:

- What methods did you use to convince your students to vote for you?

- What would you have done if you had been allowed to use any method to win?

Pre-Reading Activity: Power Plays around the World

This activity addresses power dynamics in a more explicit way. It focuses on identifying and exploring four distinct systems of power. For your convenience, a printable guide for this activity ("World Power Plays") has been provided in the Appendix.

Divide your class into four groups. Explain to the students that there are four major political systems found in the modern world. Ask students if they know of any. If so, list them on the board. The four systems you will be exploring here are: representative democracy, monarchy, military dictatorship, and socialism/communism.

Each group is responsible for identifying one country that currently operates under one political system. Take advantage of current events. (Think of countries undergoing revolutions.) Students should not only identify a country, but define the system. They should also offer a brief summary of the history of that political system in that nation. Encourage your students to use valid Internet and news sources. Afterwards, students should present their research. They can even do so in the form of a drama, acting how the political system affects the day-to-day living of the citizens of their selected country.

Reading Activity: Questions & Discussion Topics

It is very important for lessons to be rooted in the text. According to research, many students lack good textual analytical skills. To address this deficit, critical literacy, which tends to explore generative themes, must also be grounded in real textual examples. To balance these two goals, we have created both reading comprehension questions and in-class discussion topics/activities that include critical textual analysis. To serve as an example, we have provided reading comprehension questions for the first chapter of *Lord of the Flies*. We have also provided discussion topics for the entire text. To save class time, we recommend the questions be done for homework, and class time be used for the in-class discussions and activities.

Chapter: The Sound of the Shell (pp. 7–31)

1. What do we learn from the boys' conversation?

2. What is your first impression of Ralph and Piggy?

3. Why does Piggy want to organize the survivors?

4. From their conversations, what do we learn about Ralph's and Piggy's backgrounds?

5. Why does Piggy think everyone is dead?

6. What does Piggy discover? What use does he find for it?

7. Why do you think "the children gave [Piggy] the same simple obedience that they have given to other men with megaphones" (p. 18)?

8. Who is Jack? What is he the leader of?

9. The author describes Jack's group as "a party of boys, march-
   ing approximately in step in two parallel lines and dressed
   in strangely eccentric clothing" (p. 19). What image do you
   think the author is trying to evoke?

10. Even though Piggy is the most intelligent, why do the boys
    make fun of him?

11. What democratic process do the boys use to pick a chief? Who
    do they pick?

12. How do the boys divide labor? What jobs do they create?

13. Where do Simon, Ralph, and Jack go? What do they discover?

14. Why doesn't Jack, the designated hunter, kill the piglet?

In-Class Discussion: *Micro- vs. Macro-Societies*

The island represents a micro-society of the larger (macro) world.
Because the boys' experience in the "outside" world is a democracy, they attempt to recreate such a system on the island. Are
they successful? Why or why not? What is the author's opinion
of democracy? What social roles do the boys designate? What is
the author's view of law? What is the boys' view of law? What
themes or ideas does each of the boys (Ralph, Jack, Simon, Piggy,
and Roger) symbolize? When answering the above questions, use
evidence from the text to support your argument. What is *your*
opinion of democracy? Explain. Whose voice is heard in the democratic process? Whose voice is not heard? Is our country (United
States) a true representation of democracy? How can one participate in the democratic process and be heard? In what ways do the
societies that you belong to mimic larger societies (social groups,
hobby clubs, sports teams, lunch crowd, etc.)? Is there a democratic process in your own home/family, neighborhood, or within
your own social group/friends?

Chapter: Fire on the Mountain (pp. 32–47)

In-Class Discussion: *Morality: Taught or Inborn?*

How does the boys' society begin to fall apart? Why does this
happen? Do the boys still have a sense of morality? Where does
it come from? What do the boys' value? Where did their value
system and sense of morality come from? What does this tell us
about the author's view of morality? What is your view on morality? How do your views on morality differ from the dominant

(or majority) viewpoint? The teacher should have prior discussion about what is meant by "dominant culture" (refer to Chapter Two for explanation). What does the dominant society value? What are some things you value and why? How were you taught values? Do your values conflict with the dominant (or majority/mainstream) values? Why do you think certain values or morals are considered more valuable or important than others? Who determines which values or morals one should abide by? Are morals and values different depending on cultural background? Give examples.

Chapter: Huts on the Beach (pp. 48–57)

In-Class Discussion: *Loaded Leaders*

How are Jack's and Ralph's leadership styles beginning to differentiate? What two world views are they symbolic of? What two objecting life purposes do they represent? With each being a respected leader of their political system, what are their contradictory objectives for society? Who and what are they concerned with? What drives this concern? Despite the power struggle, how do the boys continue to mimic a society? What infrastructure have they created? How have they developed linguistically, technologically, etc.? Imagine that Jack and Ralph were actually two females. Do you think if these two leaders were female, their leadership styles would be different? Explain.

What qualities make a strong leader? Who, in your life, do you consider a leader and why? Think about leaders such as the president, local and state politicians, church and community leaders, or leaders in your home, neighborhood, school, or classroom. Are these leaders representing our voices and interests? Why or why not? What are some actions we can take to force our leaders to listen to our concerns and act out of our interests?

Chapter: Painted Faces and Long Hair (pp. 58–75)

In-Class Discussion: *Power Plays*

Does this society still resemble a democracy? Who has power? Who does not? How did they attain power? Who attempts to wrest power from Ralph? How does the power struggle begin? How do Simon, Ralph, Roger, Jack, and Piggy think power ought to be used? How does Jack become more savage? The fire is the boys' connection to the outside world, to the real civilization and moral code. What does it mean when the fire is extinguished? How do you define power (e.g., power through money, status, popularity or population size, knowledge, etc.)? How is the author defining power in the book? In your world (family/home, social group/friends, classroom, school, neighborhood, or church), who has power? Thinking from one of the above examples, how is that power used? What are the advantages and disadvantages of having power? Who benefits from having power, and how? Who does not benefit from having power, and why? Do you hold power in any way? Explain. If you held power, how would you use it? Should power rest in the hands of a few or shared by many? Defend your position.

Think about the choice of language and/or themes the author uses. How are characters described? What themes are found in the book that you could relate to today? For example, take the words *savagery* or *civilized* (or insert any descriptive words, themes, or dichotomies here: "good versus bad/evil," "reason versus impulse," "order versus chaos," or "law versus anarchy"). If critically examining the theme of "civilized versus savagery" and how it plays out in character development, ask students why the author associates civilized with "good" and savagery with "bad" or "evil." Other questions to consider about this theme: What comes to mind when you think of the word "savage" or "civilized" when used to describe someone? Who (person, social group) comes to mind when these words are used? Why? Do schools, society, or media play a role in perpetuating the use of these words in harmful, stereotypical, or positive ways? (Think about how these words are used in books or novels and with whom the words are often associated; or how the media casts or represents a "savage-like" or "civilized" character.) Who, typically, is not thought of, or characterized as, a "savage"? Why? Are all humans capable of acting in a "savage-like" manner? What conditions force people to act savagely or civilly? Have you ever felt the impulse to act like a "savage"? Why or why not? What prevents some people from acting savagely or civilly? Are we socially conditioned to act in certain ways? Who determines the "proper" way to act? Does this "proper" way to act conflict with your values or cultural beliefs? Is there ever justification in acting savagely? If so, does the meaning of the word "savage" change from negative to positive?

Chapter: Beast from Water (pp. 76–94)

In-Class Discussion: *The Role of Fear and Superstition in Society*

How do Jack and the hunters use fear to their advantage? How does the beast become a source of power? Who accesses this power and how? How do the boys become more and more like the beast? Again, what does this tell us about the author's view of morality? Do you agree with this view? What do you think the fear of the beast represents in our society? Think how fear can be used to persuade or pressure people into doing things they may normally not do. How is fear used to convince people that it is in their best interest to act in certain ways? Have you ever used fear to your advantage? How? Are there social or political institutions that use fear as a weapon to control or persuade? Think about institutions such as schools, the church or religion, media, government/politicians, or police/criminal justice system. Give examples.

> ### One Step Further
> Imagine that the island boys had arrived at the destination they were headed to. What would their lives be like? What would they be doing? Where would they be living? How would they be coping with the "real war"? Write a brief story describing the same characters in this situation.

Chapter: Beast from Air (pp. 95–108)

In-Class Discussion: *The Real World*

How has Ralph's power changed? Who has become more powerful? Why? The dead parachutist gives us a peek into the outside world, the "real world" beyond the island. What is going on in the world? How does it emphasize the themes playing out on the island? In bringing the war to the island, what is the author emphasizing?

Chapter: Shadows and Tall Trees (pp. 109–123)

In-Class Discussion: *Power Struggles*

Why is Ralph's enthusiasm in the hunt significant? What does the author seem to imply about human nature? How does the power struggle between Jack and Ralph escalate? How does Jack manipulate Ralph and plant seeds of distrust in his authority? How does Ralph's not seeing the beast diminish his power and authority? How does Jack's seeing the beast increase his? Think about what leadership, power, and authority means. Define each word, reflecting on how the word affects you in your everyday life. In your world, how does one acquire or lose leadership, power, or authority? Is it earned, voted upon, passed down? Who has authority in your home? Neighborhood? Peer group? School? Church? Is leadership, power, or authority held by one person, a small group of people, or a majority of people? Give examples. How can we influence change in leadership, power, or authority?

Chapter: Gift for the Darkness (pp. 124–144)

In-Class Discussion: *Understanding the Outcast*

How does belief in the beast change the dynamics of the society? What role does the Lord of the Flies play in that system? Why is

Simon's encounter with the Lord of the Flies significant? What does he realize the Lord of the Flies is? What does the Lord of the Flies symbolize? Compare Simon to Jack and Ralph. Do you think he fits in the author's broader character scheme? Explain. What social group do you think Simon represents in our world? Can you relate to any of these characters—Simon, Jack, or Ralph? Thinking of *your* life, what social group do you fit in? What made you decide which group to associate with? Was it by choice? Which social group is more popular? Powerful? What makes a particular social group more popular or powerful? What makes a particular social group less popular or powerful? Have you ever felt like you didn't belong? Was this by choice? Were you ever an outcast? Think about being an outcast in the context of peer or social group, race, culture, ethnicity, gender, sexuality, ability (disability), and even physical appearance. Who determines what is acceptable and unacceptable or popular and unpopular? Who are the outcasts in your school? Neighborhood? Larger society? How are outcasts represented in media? What do they look like? How are they perceived? Are there benefits of being an outcast? Are there benefits of being part of a social group? What are the disadvantages?

Chapter: A View of Death (pp. 145–154)

In-Class Discussion: *The Beast Within*

With Simon's barbaric murder, the island civilization unravels. Suddenly a storm ravages the island and overtakes the boys with its wildness. What is the storm symbolic of? The storm washes away all proof that the beast did not exist. Why can't Jack allow his tribe to believe that the beast is dead? How does Jack need the beast? How does the beast solidify Jack's tribe? In his barbaric murder, what beast does Simon come face-to-face with? What does the beast symbolize? Is there a beast within all of us? Explain. If students feel there is a beast within us, how do we "control" or tame this beast? How do we use it as a source of strength?

Chapter: The Shell and the Glasses (pp. 155–168)

In-Class Discussion: *Losing Sight*

Who has absolute power over the boys? How does he maintain that power? Why is the loss of Piggy's glasses and the conch so significant? What are they symbolic of? What happens to the boys' sense of morality? Can you think of another time in history when society's "conch" and "glasses" were lost? Can you think of a time in your life when the "conch" shell and "glasses" were lost? Who, in society, holds the "conch" shell? Think about this in the context of your peer group, family, school, society, church, government, corporations, or media.

Chapter: Castle Rock (pp. 169–182)

In-Class Discussion: *What Have We Become?*

Explore the boys' mental states. Do they have reason, morality, or any semblance of their "British-ness"? How does the author characterize or define "British-ness?" Is anyone on the island aware of their deterioration? What is the author trying to tell us about our society, and more importantly, about ourselves? Can you recall any historical or contemporary moments when people forgot their "British-ness" (civility) and participated in horrific acts of savagery? Now place yourself into the shoes of the people participating in the "horrific act of savagery." From the their perspective, would you describe your act as "horrific" or "savagery"? If no, how would you describe it (as justice, revolutionary, protest, rebellious)? The point here is to play on the notion of how words carry power in describing people (or events, history, etc.) and how the use of words can influence and perpetuate certain ideologies over others (a powerful form of how hegemony operates).

Chapter: Cry of the Hunters (pp. 183–202)

In-Class Discussion: *Rescued from Ourselves*

What kind of fire catches the attention of the rescue ship? Why is this ironic? What is the author trying to tell us about the relationship of civilization and war? Why is it ironic that the officer can-

---

One Step Further

In a writing assignment, have your students consider how they treat and are treated by people from other class structures. Some questions to explore:

- How is difference dealt with in school? Does your teacher tolerate opposing opinions? Why or why not?
- How is difference dealt with at home? Do your parents/guardians tolerate opposing opinions? Explain.
- How is difference dealt within your social group? Do your friends tolerate opposing opinions? Why or why not?
- How is difference dealt with in media (television shows, films, or music videos)? How are certain groups—based on social class (or race or gender)—portrayed in media? How is your "group" (based on race, class, gender) generally represented or treated in media?
- How do you deal with difference? What political system are you? Are you a representative democracy, a monarchy, a military dictatorship, or a social communist?

not understand the boys' behavior? The teacher can expand this topic to examine more critically the concept of war. How do students define "war"? Who are the parties involved in a war? Could it be between friends, family, neighborhoods, states, or countries? Can wars occur between different socioeconomic (class), cultural, or gender backgrounds? Give examples of each. Can wars be civilized? Or is it instinctual to act in a primal, savage manner?

Post-Reading Activity: Got Class?

For this activity, revisit the four political systems your students presented in the Pre-Reading Activity in an exciting new way. For your convenience, a printable guide for this activity ("School Social Pyramid") has been provided in the Appendix.

For homework, have your students identify the various social classes at your school. Encourage them to look around the cafeteria, at their own lunch table, and identify the various groups they participate and do not participate in. Consider the various groups' mannerisms, including the way they speak, interests, and even clothing. Ask your students to create their own school social hierarchy. Which group is at the top of the pyramid? Which group is at the bottom? Why? Does each group have a leader? What distinguishes the leader from other group members?

To begin a conversation in class, have students hand in their pyramid worksheets (this should be done anonymously). Post them on the board gallery style. Have students walk around and observe the different systems. Then, talk about the similarities and differences of the pyramids. What do the pyramids reveal about your school and the importance of class and perspective? How are these social classes symbolic of larger societal trends? Is it possible to resist class? How can we tear down any existing hierarchies in our world/school/neighborhood? What are the benefits of doing so?

Text 2: *Push* by Sapphire (1996)

Unlike the *Lord of the Flies*, the lesson plan on *Push* is designed inward-out, beginning with a personal view and moving to a broader study on issues of class and survival. In this unit, we also try take it a step further by exploring how social class has very real effects on individual lives.

Lesson Opener: Power Walk

This assignment is designed to help students become aware of what they are already most familiar with: their surroundings. For your convenience, a printable guide for this activity ("Power Walk") has been provided in the Appendix. Two versions are available: one to analyze New York City subway stops (feel free to revise to reflect your location), and another to analyze the neighborhood.

What Is *Push* About?

Push tells the story of Claireece Precious Jones, an illiterate African American teenager who is determined to break out of her crippling circumstances. Growing up in Harlem, Precious is socially invisible, having two children by her father before the age of 18, being continuously abused by her unstable mother, and receiving an A in English even though she cannot read. In a stroke of luck, Precious finds herself in an alternative education program with a teacher who refuses to let her give in or give up. Ultimately, Precious finds her freedom and discovers her voice in literacy. Told in stirring, and at times, explosive, prose and poetry, *Push* inspires the reader to *push* on and overcome any life situation.

For this assignment, have your students take a Power Walk around their hometown. Explain that they will be working in pairs, as investigative journalists, writing an article on the state of the local metro system or their neighborhood (this can be adapted to suit your local area). Assign your students specific subways stops or locations to visit in their community, some in the wealthy areas and others in the poorer parts of town.

If possible, provide each team with a disposable camera with which they can document their findings (or encourage your students to use digital/phone cameras). You can also do this activity by assigning each group a different focus (one group can cover the subway stations, another parks, another local businesses, etc.). After all the information has been collected, groups can share their field notes and mark on a large map the locations they found to be in the best and worst conditions. After all this information is mapped, encourage a discussion on why the facilities of certain areas are more neglected than others.

Pre-Reading Activity: The Power to Be the Best Version of Me

This activity turns the attention closer towards the theme of *Push*, resisting class. These poems represent different voices in different circumstances. For your convenience, a printable guide for this activity ("The Road to Me") has been provided in the Appendix.

In class, either assign different students to read aloud different poems or song lyrics, or have students work through all of them in small groups. Some works we suggest: "Invictus" by William Ernest Henley; "The Show Goes On" by Lupe Fiasco; "Defeat" by Edgar Guest; "Stupid Girls" by Pink; "Don't Quit," Anonymous; "Born This Way" by Lady Gaga; "I Can" by Nas; "Hey Young

World" by Slick Rick; "Hey Young World: Part 2" by Macy Gray. Or use your students as experts and ask them to bring in poems or printed lyrics that reflect the theme of staying true to yourself and resisting mainstream pressures to conform.

In conversation, compare and contrast the authors' voices, and where applicable, discuss how class affected their personal struggle. Afterwards, ask your students where they envision themselves in ten years. They can record these visions either by drawing a self-portrait or by completing the road map guide. If they are using the road map, have them consider when they will begin this journey, what steps they will take, and what road blocks they will need to overcome. (We encourage you to complete this activity as well. Not only will you effectively model the activity, but you will be entering the conversation as a real participant, not just as an authority.) These works can then be shared with the class in a gallery walk. You can also encourage your students to keep their maps/portraits in a convenient location to constantly remind themselves of their long-term goals.

Cultural Literacy: Bi-dialectical Teaching Opportunity

Push is an excellent example of how language, particularly dialect, can be examined from a critical perspective. Have discussions prior to and throughout the reading to explore language and dialect use. Cultural literacy is important here, especially when contrasting this book with "classical" literature such as *Lord of the Flies* to examine how language and dialects are used to legitimize certain cultures and groups over others. Critical in understanding cultural literacy is the teacher's understanding and familiarization of particular dialects used in texts—in this case, Ebonics. Remember from Chapter Two that language and dialect are intricately tied to one's cultural identity; therefore, if we label a particular dialect as inferior, we are ultimately sending a message that the person speaking that dialect is inferior.

The dialect used in *Push* is spoken by many African Americans and is referred to as either "African American Vernacular English," "Black English," or "Ebonics." According to sociolinguists, these names have been used interchangeably (we will refer to it as Ebonics). According to the Linguistic Society of America, Ebonics "is systematic and rule-governed like all natural speech varieties . . . . The systematic and expressive nature of the grammar and pronunciation patterns of the African-American vernacular has been established by numerous scientific studies over the past thirty years. Characterizations of Ebonics as 'slang,' 'mutant,' 'lazy,' 'defective,' 'ungrammatical,' or 'broken English' are incorrect and demeaning" (Linguistic Society of America, 1998, p. 160). Common grammatical patterns spoken from Ebonics speakers are "(1) aspectual 'be'; (2) stressed 'been'; (3) multiple negations; (4) adjacency/context in possessives; (5) postvocalic /r/ deletion; (6) copula absence; and (7) camouflaged and other unique lexical forms" (Smitherman, 1998, p. 31). We emphasize again the importance of teachers researching on their own specific grammatical patterns and examples found in Ebonics prior to engaging students in the reading of *Push*.

After having a discussion on Standard American English and its dialects (discussed in Chapter Two), here are some cultural-literacy questions to consider with your students:

1. Since the book is written in first-person narrative, what do you notice about the language, terms, and phrases that are used? Have students browse through the book, flipping through pages, and write down unique word or phrases that are used.

2. What dialect is the speaker using? (Ebonics, African American Vernacular, Black English. It's important to clarify these terms to your students and refrain from using descriptors such as "broken English," "slang," or any other negative label associated with the dialect of Ebonics.)

3. Say some of the words or phrases aloud. Listen to how the words sound. Do you know someone who speaks or sounds like the speaker in the text? If so, who? (The teacher could give examples of famous literary authors or poets who write in this dialect—Zora Neale Hurston, Toni Morrison, Langston Hughes, or other famous and successful Americans such as Charles Barkley, Lil Wayne, Jay-Z, Steve Harvey, Mo'Nique—all of whom employ Ebonics on occasion.)

4. How do you think people who do not speak in the dialect of Ebonics perceive Ebonics speakers? And where does this perception come from?

5. How does the media influence your perception of Ebonics speakers?

6. Imagine if the book *Push* were written using a different dialect, or in Standard American English. Would your perception of the characters change? Would the setting change?

7. Is there a "correct," "proper," or "standard" way of speaking? Dressing? Acting? If yes, why? And if yes, in which context is it appropriate? Who sets the standard?

8. If yes to question #7, who determines the "proper" or "correct" way to speak, dress, or act? Does it have to do with race, social class, or power/status? Explain and give examples.

9. What is "code-switching"? And why do we need to code-switch? Do all people feel it necessary to code-switch or does it depend on social class, power, or status?

Activities: Dialect Detectives

Tell students they will be Dialect Detectives who must bring in evidence of the ways in which people talk differently. Media texts like radio, news reporters and anchors, or television and films can be great sources. It can be useful to interview people who speak differently as well. Students learn to understand that although we may sound different or speak in another dialect, we can still understand each other. Dialectical diversity exists and is tied to one's identity. The goal here is to promote acceptance— and celebration—of differences.

Ask students to bring in printed and audio/electronic versions of lyrics that reflect different dialects. Students can work in small groups to look for particular speech patterns heard or viewed (in printed form) in the lyrics. Ask students to translate—in writing—the dialect into Standard American English. Or ask the students to explain—in writing—the message or themes found in the lyrics using Standard American English. This can be done in essays or poetry. Students can write a response to the author (artist) of the lyrics using Standard American English or using their own dialect. Take an excerpt from *Lord of the Flies* or other classical text using Standard American English and ask students to translate it in their own dialect. In this activity, to prevent the reverence or superiority of one dialect as the "correct" or "proper" dialect over another, it's important to include opportunities for students to write in different dialects. Students can create bi-dialectical dictionaries or thesauruses using their own dialect and Standard American English.

Students can engage in role-playing, performance arts/theatre, or spoken-word poetry to teach code-switching without denigrating home dialects. Some students are brilliantly skilled at imitating others. Acting from a different persona allows students to freely and comfortably code-switch without fear of being corrected or ridiculed by their peers or teacher. Ask students to play the role of a news anchor to report local happenings in the school or community.

Reading Activity: Questions & Discussion Topics

It is very important for lessons to be rooted in the text. According to research, many students lack good textual analytical skills. To address this deficit, critical literacy, which tends to explore generative themes, must also be grounded in real textual examples. To balance these two goals, we have created both reading comprehension questions and in-class discussion topics/activities that include critical textual analysis. To encourage your own growth as an educator, comprehension questions have only been provided for Part 1. We have also provided discussion topics for the entire text. To save class time, we recommend the questions be answered as homework, and class time be used for the in-class discussions and activities. Because of the personal nature of the discussion topics, you may want to consider giving students time to reflect in a reading log, private diary, or allowing them to express themselves through poetry, song, or art.

Part 1 (pp. 3–33)

1. When does the story begin? Where does *Push* take place?

2. Reading just the first page, how would you describe Precious' voice? What information does it provide us with?

3. What effect does the author's writing style have on you as a reader?

4. What happened to Precious' first baby?

5. Why can't Precious turn to the correct page of her math book?

6. Why do you think Precious keeps "law and order" in Mr. Wicher's class (p. 6)?

7. Why does Precious get suspended? Do you think the school's policy is fair? Explain.

8. What do you think of Mrs. Lichtenstein? Do you think she really wants to help Precious? Does she? Why or why not?

9. What happened when Precious' mother found out she was pregnant the first time?

10. Why is Precious attracted to the paramedic who takes her to the hospital? What does it tell us about her life?

11. What happened when the nurse realized that Precious was just 12-years old? Does she help her?

12. How long has Precious been abused? Does she realize she's being abused? How does she deal with her situation?

13. Who are "the men in uniform suits" (p. 13)? Why doesn't Precious tell them anything?

14. Why doesn't Precious' mother allow Mrs. Lichtenstein in the house?

15. Where does Mrs. Lichtenstein suggest Precious go? How does Precious feel about it?

In-Class Discussion: *"Push, Precious, you gonna hafta Push. . . . "*

The theme of the book is *push.* It's not easy for Precious to break out of her reality. She needs to push (like the babies she pushes out of her womb) in order to become the person she wants to be. How do you motivate yourself when things get tough? What pushes you to be a better person?

16. What condition was Precious' first child born with? Do you think she and her mother understand the condition? How do they treat Little Mongo?

17. Where does Little Mongo live? Why does Precious' mother tell the welfare agents that she's living with them?

18. What happens when Precious' mother finds out that Carl has been raping Precious?

In-Class Discussion: *Dealing with Pain*

How does Precious deal with her pain? Do you think this way is healthy? Why or why not? What are some unhealthy ways people deal with pain? How do you deal with pain? What are some ways to deal with pain in a healthier way? This discussion provides a great opportunity to incorporate popular culture into the lesson (e.g., dealing with pain through lyrics/music, online web forums, social networking sites, etc).

19. Why does Precious' mother abuse her? Are there other forms of abuse? By whom?

20. Who is Farrakhan? Why does he inspire Precious? Who is someone who inspires you?

21. How has Precious' situation worsened?

22. Why is Precious confused by her father's abuse? Why does she blame herself?

23. Why is Precious upset about her file? What is she worried about?

24. Precious thinks she'll be in the GED class because she was in ninth grade. Is she? What does this tell us about the schools Precious has been attending?

25. How does Precious do on the evaluation tests? How does she feel about her score?

26. How does Precious feel about herself? Why do you think she's come to see herself in this way?

In-Class Discussion: *Tests*

When Precious does poorly on the placement test, she is not surprised. She tells us: "For me this nuffin' new. There has always been something wrong wif the tesses. The tesses paint a picture of me wif no brain. The tesses paint a picture of me an' my muver—my whole family, we more than dumb, we invisible" (p. 30). What does Precious mean that the tests "paint a picture of [her without a] brain"? Do you think Precious is right? Why or why not? Do tests "paint a picture" of one's family or background? How? Do you think Precious is dumb? Why or why not? What does Precious mean when she says the tests make her family "invisible"? Do you think if Precious came from a different social class or racial background, she would perform better on tests? Would she be perceived differently? Why or why not? Did you ever feel "invisible"? Explain. How do you feel about taking placement exams or standardized tests? What do the tests "say" about you or your family?

Part 2 (pp. 34–66)

In-Class Discussion: *Education vs. Schooling*

On page 57, Precious writes that she's "got no education even tho' [she's] not miss day of school." Is this possible? Explain. What does *education* mean to you? Is it achieved by going to school each day? Explain the difference between being "schooled" and being "educated." Are some people being "schooled" and others being "educated"? Who are these people? Is it based on race, class, gender differences? How do you feel about your education? Do you feel you are truly learning new material that will be useful in your life? Does the curriculum in your classes represent, mis-represent, or under-represent *you*? How about your culture? Your gender? Your ethnicity? Your race? In what ways? How much time is spent in school covering your racial, cultural, ethnic, or class background (in *all* of your subjects)? What topics are covered that reflect your background in each subject area? Do students from different backgrounds gain a clear understanding of your back-ground when or if it's studied in the curriculum? What perception or knowledge do you have of others who are different from you? What can teachers do to ensure all students are receiving a quality education? What can *you* do to ensure this?

In-Class Discussion: *A Precious Little Change*

What does Precious realize about the abuse she's been through? Who does she blame for what happened to her? What gives her the courage to face her past? How does Precious begin to break away and differentiate herself from the world she grew up in? What are the tools that help her do this? Have you ever been in a situation that you needed to change or get out of? If yes, share (if you feel comfortable) how you coped with the situation and how it was resolved. This can be completed in either written (private diary) or discussion format. What are other forms of abuse (emo-tional, mental, physical)? Who has the power to abuse (friends, family, partner, authority figures, leaders, police, teachers, etc.)? Put yourself in the shoes of someone who has been abused (men-tally, physically, or emotionally) and write from that person's per-spective. Now write from the abuser's perspective.

Part 3 (pp. 67–97)

In-Class Discussion: *"I Think I Might Be the Solution"*

On page 75, Precious tells us: The "skinny, black [nurse] . . . say she sorry to see me back here, and hoped I be done learned from my mistakes. What kinda shit is that! I didn't make no mistakes unless it being born, n' Miz Rain say I was born for a purpose, 'n Mr. Wicher has said I had aptitude in maff. I don't know what purpose, but I know I got a purpose, a reason. . . . Mistake? I don't think so. Mistakes for niggers to rape. I think I might be the solution." Who does the nurse think is responsible for Precious' situation? How does it affect her actions? What about this episode makes Precious believe that she has a purpose? What is she the solution to? What is your purpose? What are you the solution of? What obstacles are in your way to prevent finding a solution or purpose? Does being from a particular race, social class, or gender make it easier to reach your purpose? If the character of Precious was a boy rather than a girl, how does this change the story (besides the obvious of getting pregnant)? Or, perhaps if the main character was a boy, how does the story change if the boy got a girl pregnant? If the story was about a male being raped and abused by his mother *or* father, would it change your perception of the male character? Are there double standards for male victims versus female victims when we think about abuse? Are there stereotypes associated with these roles? If so, where do you think they come from? How can we address and rectify them?

In-Class Discussion: *Road Map of Life*

At the halfway house, Precious is told that she is, "Halfway between the life you had and the life you want" (p. 84). Right now in high school, you are also half way between the life you have and the life you want to have. Reflect on the road map you made in the pre-reading activity. Reflect on this particular chapter of your road map. What does your halfway house look like? How can we learn to better deal with the difficulties this stage presents? What factors or conditions are in place that make it difficult or challenging to reach the life you want? Does your race, class, gender, sexuality, or language factor into achieving the life you want? Explain.

In-Class Discussion: *Dark Holes*

On page 87, Precious tells us, "I got Alice Walker up there with Harriet Tubman n' Farrakhan. But she can't help me now. Where my *Color Purple*? Where my god most high? Where my king? Where my black love? Where my man love? Woman love? Any kinda love? Why me? I don't deserve this. I not crack addict. Why I get Mama for a mama? Why I not born a light-skin dream? Why? Why?" Put yourself in Precious' shoes—describe your feelings. Have you ever felt similar feelings of pain and frustration? Did you ever wish you could be someone else or have a different life, family, or friends? What if Precious was from a wealthy family, do you think she would face similar problems? Why do you think Precious can't believe that she is HIV-positive? According to her, who usually gets HIV? This revelation has the potential to destroy Precious' life. How does she overcome the urge to sink into a

> ### One Step Further
> Why does Precious choose to read a poem by Langston Hughes? What is the significance of her choice? Read the poem through Precious' eyes. How does it reflect her journey? What does it tell us about her motivation?

dark hole? Have you ever faced a dark hole? If you have, how did you get through it?

Part 4 (pp. 98–140)

In-Class Discussion: *Different Agendas*

Precious and her friends are convinced that Ms. Weiss (Meaning "white" in German) wants all of them to prepare to enter the workforce and perform menial, demeaning labor. Do you think they are right or wrong? Explain why. Do you think society has a plan for people like Precious? Do you think we are assigned specific jobs or paths in life? If yes, are these paths determined by race, class, or gender? Does physical appearance, language difference, or ability level determine one's path in life? Do teachers, schools, communities play a role in determining one's path? Does economic status play a role in affecting the path we take? What does the author believe? What agenda do Precious and her friends have? How do they challenge the role they believe society has assigned to them?

Analyze different forms of media (television, films, videos, commercials, and advertisements) and examine how diverse groups of people are portrayed. Do you see patterns based on race, class, ethnicity, gender, or sexuality? Name some stereotypes often depicted in media. Students can look at how African Americans, Italian Americans, Asian Americans, Muslim Americans, and others are represented, or misrepresented, in media. An interesting example is analyzing reality television that draws on specific themes based on age, race, ethnicity, and class (e.g., the Real World series, *The Jersey Shore*, *Keeping Up with the Kardashians*, or the Real Housewives franchise of New Jersey, New York, Atlanta, Orange County, or Beverly Hills). Who is missing from these shows? How is gender defined? How are roles defined? How are relationships defined (i.e., heterosexual versus homosexual representations)? How much responsibility do the "actors" or "reality stars" have in portraying themselves in a particular manner? What is the responsibility of the network and sponsors who are capitalizing on huge profits on the show(s)? What role do the writers, producers, directors, or editors of the show have in representing characters? What role do we, as consumers of the product, have on the show's popularity?

In-Class Discussion: *Precious Tyger*

Compare Precious' poem to William Blake's "The Tyger." How does the author (also a poet) reinvent the poem? Assuming all art is in dialogue, a big conversation with one another, what is the message of Blake's poem? How is Precious' critical of his ideas?

In-Class Discussion: *Precious Reborn*

After meeting her mother, Precious tells us: "something tear inside me. I wanna cry but I can't cry. I think how *alive* I am, every part of me that is cells, proteens, neutrons, hairs, pussy, eyeballs, nervus system, brain. I got poems, a son, friends. I want to live so bad" (p. 137). Why do you think Precious describes her feelings this way? What has changed for her? How is Precious *reborn*? Compare and contrast Precious' "spiritual rescue" to how the boys in the *Lord of the Flies* are physically rescued. How did Precious overcome her own struggles? Have you ever been in a situation that required rescue? What kind of rescue was it? Who helped you? Did you want their help? How did you get through your tough times?

One Step Further

Because learning is only meaningful when it touches our own lives, encourage your students to write their life story in a Precious-like free-style verse, or in the student's home dialect. Publish these works in a class book. To encourage pride, there are a number of places to get your book inexpensively published such as www.studentpublishing.com. Creating a book will encourage your students to understand and tolerate their fellow classmates, fostering a sense of community while empowering their individual voices.

Post-Reading Activity: *Write Your Life Story*

For your convenience, a printable guide for this activity ("Where Is She Now?") has been provided in the Appendix.

Read the last section of *Push*, "Life Stories," together. Discuss the girls' different stories and the various ways they reflect and cope with their past. Then, have your students write the future chapters of Precious' life. Allow your students to freely imagine what will happen to Precious. After they work through the "Where Is She Now" guide, place their stories in chronological order and post them on the board. Afterwards, discuss with your students what choices Precious had to make to arrive at the different points. For example, if one student imagines Precious will be a doctor in ten years and another thinks she will become a drug addict, place both on the board and examine the different choices and circumstances that may lead to those possibilities.

To stimulate further discussion, refer to the "Critical Literacy/ Critical Textual Analysis" guide, paying particular attention to the "Reconstructing the text" section when completing the last activity. Changing certain aspects of the story can bring about thoughtful, critical debate about diverse issues that hit close to home with your students. After the final chapters have been written, ask students to share their endings in small groups and select one ending to share with the larger class. After reaching a consensus as to which story ending will be presented to the entire class, encourage students to use creative means of sharing the ending. This could be in the format of a group role-play or performance through song, the spoken word, or visual arts, such as a collage or mural that "tells" the story. Or students can create a PowerPoint or other technology-based presentation that shares their ending of the story.

CHAPTER FIVE

Race Wars

A Step from Heaven with a Part-Time Indian

I used to think the world was broken down by tribes . . . by black and white. By Indian and white. But I know that isn't true. The world is only broken down into two tribes: The people who are assholes and the people who aren't.
— Junior in *The Absolutely True Diary of a Part-Time Indian* (Alexie, 2007, p. 176)

Education either functions as an instrument which is used to facilitate integration of the younger generation into the logic of the present system and bring about conformity or it becomes the practice of freedom, the means by which men and women deal critically and creatively with reality and discover how to participate in the transformation of their world. (Freire, 1970/2000, p. 34)

Why Talk About Race?

What is America? What does it mean to be an American? Although the United States of America is a country made up of millions of different kinds of people, we tend to think of American identity as a single phenomenon as simple as apple pie. In reality, American identity or, more accurately, *identities*, is/are complex and fluid, speaking to the different experiences of millions of citizens. It is time to resist this great American myth and recognize that our national identity is forged by a vast collection of interwoven identities, histories, and truths.

If we fail to recognize these many different stories, we risk creating imbalances of power; we can even risk developing racist ways of thinking. Though racism is a multifaceted socially constructed concept, caused, transmitted, and metamorphosed in many ways, here we define it as inequality, access to power that is, unintentionally or not, denied to a group of people. This limited access to power can touch political, economic, and social spheres. A few examples of potential issues of racism in schools include student government representation; unfair grouping on sports teams; and marginal, inaccurate, or distorted representations in the curriculum.

Critical pedagogues believe that we all participate in some form of power struggle, but critical pedagogy recognizes how oppressive forms of power operate and benefit. As Paulo Freire maintained, a critical pedagogy works to expose and name power constructs such as "socioeconomic class elitism, Eurocentric ways of viewing the world, patriarchal oppressions, and imperialism around the world (Kincheloe, 2008, p. 34). Whether we are positioned within the minority or majority, critical literacy advocates for the correction of power imbalances to ensure that all voices are equally heard and fairly represented. For most of us, racial thinking is unconscious and requires only recognition to be remedied. For others, it is deeply ingrained and must be explored and refuted. Either way, critical literacy promotes that teachers, who are always in positions of authority, avoid equalizing their students by granting them "freedom" to speak and act. This simply replicates the existing power structure. Instead, educators should relinquish as much of their authority as possible and serve as "facilitator" or dialectical authority by engaging their students in authentic conversation (ibid.). By taking a more receptive, facilitating role, teachers will be able to really listen to their students' existing voices and incorporate their students' knowledge or expertise into the curriculum; this will ultimately foster opportunities of empowerment, liberation, and agency (activism).

Race is something every teacher is aware of, but never wants to discuss. Why? For some, it's about avoiding an uncomfortable issue, a "p.c." thing. For others, it's the trouble of identifying and dealing with an explosive volcano, one with unpredictable capacity and range. In our experience, racism, especially at the secondary level, is an unavoidable reality. And while often pigeonholed to one or two minority groups, racism, a lack of access to power, is something that affects many students from all racial and ethnic backgrounds throughout their lives. To help get you to expand your notion of racism, this unit centers on two very different types of books. The first is *A Step from Heaven*, by An Na (2001), a personal account of a Korean American girl's immigration to the

U.S. The other, *The Absolutely True Diary of a Part-Time Indian*, by Sherman Alexie (2007), is the illustrated memoir of a Spokane Indian boy who leaves the reservation to join a "white" school.

How Do I Use This Unit?

This unit attempts to address racial inequalities through the lens of identity. By focusing on the complexity of identity, specifically the firsthand experiences of young people, students have a means through which to personally connect and explore inequalities of power. For example, in *A Step from Heaven,* Young Ju arrives in the U.S. filled with many expectations, only to find out how much she will struggle to feel American. Over time, she confronts and challenges the inequality she experiences not only as a foreigner, but as a woman as well.

The Absolutely True Diary of a Part-Time Indian also documents a young person's struggle with inequality, specifically as he tries to integrate into "mainstream" American society. Sherman Alexie's hero is a Native American, a stranger in his own homeland. Junior must leave the "rez," a place where he does not belong, and join a white suburban school, where he also does not belong, in order to find himself. Unlike most texts read in high schools, *The Absolutely True Diary of a Part-Time Indian* is very visual, filled with Junior's humorous and enlightening cartoons. This makes it not only a refreshing read to most students, but also provides an additional layer of analysis, giving students an opportunity to develop their visual literacy skills.

If *A Step from Heaven* is already on your school's reading list, we recommend teaching these books consecutively. *The Absolutely True Diary of a Part-Time Indian* is short, humorous, and thought-provoking, and can easily tie into a larger unit on immigration, racism, and/or identity. To conclude the unit, we recommend a whole-class reading of Shaun Tan's pictorial masterpiece, *The Arrival.*

Unit Opener: Addressing English Language Learners (ELLs) & Non-ELLs

This activity ultimately fosters awareness and celebration of cultural identity and linguistic diversity. Have students read any of the following short stories and poems: "Mother Tongue" by Amy Tan; "Aria" by Richard Rodriguez; "From the Woman Warrior" by Maxine Hong Kingston; "Learning Silence" by Maria Mazziotti Gillan; "Prospectus" by Joe Nieto; "Cut into Me" by Carole Yazzie-Shaw; "Mi Problema" by Michele M. Serros; "No Questions Asked" by Armand Garnet Ruffo; and "Elena" by Pat Mora.

These readings feature a variety of ethnic perspectives, but all have similar themes relating to how society shapes cultural and linguistic identities. Prolific writers and poets from various cultural and linguistic backgrounds (Chinese, Native American, Spanish and Mexican) describe the process of learning the English language and the struggles they encountered with natives from their homeland and/or with native English speakers or American society. These stories and poems provoke a profound sense of belonging—and exclusion—from both the ELLs' home culture and the dominant (American) culture. The struggle between "fitting in" the new culture yet remaining "true" to one's cultural roots, resulting in a feeling of "fitting in nowhere" is a common experience for ELLs and students with mixed-racial roots (biracial or multiracial students). Students can discuss powerful messages of how race, class, and gender are situated in the new environment or culture. ELLs in your class can be asked to share their feelings and experiences if they are comfortable doing so. Students can work in small groups to share their feelings and then report to the larger group. Alternatively, students can work with partners and interview each other about their experiences of marginalization, exclusion, and belonging. The interviewer summarizes the interviewee's responses and shares them with the larger group.

The two following books are excellent resources for incorporating themes of identity: *Identity Lessons: Contemporary Writing about Learning to Be American* (Gillan & Gillan, 1999) and *Tongue-Tied: The Lives of Multilingual Children in Public Education* (Santa Ana, 2004). Both contain short stories and poems from multiple ethnic perspectives centered on cultural and linguistic identity.

Text 1: *A Step from Heaven* by An Na

A Step from Heaven is a common secondary school text. By focusing on the broader themes of Young Ju's story, specifically her struggle to integrate into a new society, we hope to make her journey more applicable and meaningful to students.

What Is *A Step from Heaven* About?

A Step from Heaven tells the story of Young Ju, a young Korean girl who immigrates with her family to America. As she travels to America, Young Ju expects to arrive in a magical and mystical land. Instead, she is greeted by the harsh reality of immigration, forced to learn a new language, a new culture, and a new way of viewing the world. Though her journey is filled with ups and downs, it ultimately empowers her to overcome these difficulties and forever change her and her family's future.

Lesson Opener: My America

For your convenience, a printable guide for this activity ("My America") has been provided in the Appendix.

For this activity, collect a variety of images that commonly signify America and being an American. For example, apple pie, a baseball field, hot dogs, cowboys, jeans, pickup truck, the Brooklyn Bridge, Coca Cola, or a bald eagle. Present these images to your class (either as a whole or by giving each group a packet) and ask them what these images have in common. (If you have the technological capability, you can also show "American"-themed advertisements like Ford car commercials).

After students recognize that these images are used to represent American culture, have them work through the accompanying guide. Among other things, it will prompt them to respond to these images by asking how many of them have ever eaten homemade apple pie or seen a bald eagle. Depending on your student population, you will find that a number of your American students have never done these so-called American things. In small groups or as a class, discuss and explore:

- What images are commonly associated with America?

- Is the America that we see depicted on television, in the movies, and in magazines the America you live in? Why or why not?

- What does your America look like?

- What does being an American mean to you?

- How does mainstream society define an American?

- What are some of the qualities or characteristic traits that define an American?

- What makes a person "un-American"?

Following this, have students create and present their own set of American icons. Each student should explain why their objects mean "America" to them. In a gallery walk, have students explore and respond to the different Americas. Discuss this diversity and why America means so many different things to so many different people. Hang these pictures in your classroom near your American flag to remind your students what being an American means to them. Recent immigrants, ELLs, and students born outside the

U.S. who are aware of their cultural heritage should be encouraged to bring in, or draw, the flag of their country of origin. Their homeland's flag could be hung near the American flag to remind students of the great diversity that exists in and makes up America.

> **One Step Further**
> After seeing the many versions of the American dream, have students write a short essay exploring the different versions of the American dream.

Pre-Reading Activity: Statue of Liberty vs. Angel Island

By comparing the poems inscribed on the walls of Angel Island with the one engraved on the base of the Statue of Liberty, this activity explores different immigration experiences. For your convenience, a printable guide for this activity ("Interpreting the American Dream") has been provided in the Appendix.

Begin by explaining that since the mid-eighteenth century, immigrants have flooded American shores. Why do people risk so much (at times, even their lives) just to make it to American soil? Ask students to think about what immigration feels like from the perspective of immigrants. How do you think it feels to enter a new country, culture, language system? Have them brainstorm potential problems that could occur when arriving in their new land (language and communication difficulties and cultural, racial, and religious intolerance). If you have ELLs or immigrants in your class, ask if they are willing to share firsthand experiences of coming to a new country and/or learning a new language. A follow up to this activity is inviting guest speakers who are immigrants or ELLs to share their experiences and reasons for leaving their home country to start a new life in America.

Explain that the following activity explores the American dream and presents various challenges posed to the American dream. Either on the board, in conversation, or in their individual reading logs, have your students respond to the following questions:

- What is the American dream?

- How is it depicted in the media?

- Do you believe that everyone shares the same dream? Why or why not?

- Are you living the American dream? Why or why not?

Either in small groups or as a class, read "The New Colossus" by Emma Lazarus, and "There are tens of thousands of poems on these walls" by an anonymous Chinese immigrant. Compare and contrast how these two poets viewed America and the American dream. Explore how the location of these two poems speaks to the authors' individual experiences and perhaps shaped their very different views of America. In groups or in pairs, have your students complete the guide.

> ### One Step Further
> Have students read Allen Ginsberg's poem "America" and discuss their thoughts on the following themes: identity, oppression, capitalism, sexuality. Ginsberg struggled with his identity and resisted pressure to adhere to the dominant culture's narrow definition of what a male should be. A brief biographical sketch of Ginsberg's life should be read prior to discussing the poem.

Reading Activity: Questions & Discussion Topics

It is very important for lessons to be rooted in the text. According to research, many students lack good textual analytical skills. To address this deficit, critical literacy, which tends to explore generative themes, must also be grounded in real textual examples. To balance these two goals, we have created both reading comprehension questions and in-class discussion topics/activities that include critical textual analysis. To encourage your own growth as an educator, comprehension questions have only been provided for Part 1. We have also provided discussion topics for the entire text. To save class time, we recommend the questions be done for homework, and class time be used for the in-class discussions and activities. Because of the personal nature of the discussion topics, you may want to consider giving students time to reflect in a reading log or private diary.

Part 1: Thinking of America (pp. 7–23)

Chapter: *Sea Bubble*

1. About how old you think Young Ju is when the story begins?

2. Where is Young Ju when the story opens?

Chapter: *All That Weight*

1. Who is Apa? Uhmma? Halmoni? Harabugi?

2. Why are Young Ju's parents unhappy?

3. What happens "when Apa comes home late stinking like the insides of the bottles that get left on the street" (p. 8)?

Chapter: *Only God Can*

1. Why does Halmoni tell Young Ju to pray?

2. Where does Young Ju think heaven is? Why does she think this?

3. What does Young Ju ask her harabugi to ask God? Why?

Chapter: *Mi Gook*

1. Where is Mi Gook? Why is it a "magic word" (p. 11)?

2. What do Young Ju's relatives from America send her? What does she think of the gifts?

3. What does Young Ju's family tell her Mi Gook is like?

4. Why does Ju Mi refuse to play with Young Ju? Why do you think she feels betrayed?

5. What is Young Ju worried about when she hears her family is moving?

In-Class Discussion: America = Heaven?

Where does Young Ju think Mi Gook is? What are her expectations? What type of metaphor is the author creating here? Why? What is she trying to tell us about fantasies in general and fantasies about America in particular?

Chapter: *Hair*

1. Why do Young Ju and her mother get all dressed up?

2. Why does Young Ju get her hair curled? Does she want her hair curled? Why or why not?

3. How does Young Ju feel about her curly hair?

Chapter: *Waiting for Heaven*

1. What is the "bus that bounces and rolls like a boat on stormy waters" (p. 21)?

2. What does Halmoni mean when she tells Young Ju that "Mi Gook is only for young people to have a new start . . . not for old people who are used-up dry fishbones" (p. 21)?

3. What is the "thick rope holding [Young Ju] down [to her seat]" (p. 22)?

In-Class Discussion: New Experiences

To Young Ju, everything seems strange and unknown. She believes the airplane is a bus, her seatbelt is a rope, and she doesn't even realize that she's hiding in the bathroom. Have you ever had an experience where you felt like an outsider, like everyone around you understood something that you did not? How did you realize that you were "out of the loop"?

Part 2: Becoming American (pp. 28–81)

In-Class Discussion: *Gender Roles/Gender Rules*

In Young Ju's family, who makes the major family decisions? What happens when someone objects or questions the decision? How does Apa treat Uhmma? Compare how Apa treats the women in his life to the men in his life (namely Joon). What does Apa believe the respective roles of men and women are? What do you think informed his opinion? Do you agree or disagree? Explain. Have you ever felt that you've been treated differently because of your gender? Explain. Does your family have specific expectations for you because you are a man or a woman? Do gender roles differ depending on cultural background? Share. Do you feel your parents, friends, or teachers treat boys and girls differently? How so? Do you agree or disagree with such practices? Explain. Where do gender roles or expectations come from? When, and from whom, do we learn them? Do you feel pressured or obligated to act in certain ways around the same sex? Opposite sex? Do media have influence in promoting gender roles?

Activity: *How to Build a Gender Stereotype*

Analyze popular television shows and films that perpetuate stereotypical gender roles. Point out some shows that challenge gender stereotyping. Utilize students as a resource of knowledge. Ask them to name some shows or films that reflect this theme. Choose one show or film to focus on and consider the following questions: What role or position do men and women play in the show/film? How are the male and female characters portrayed? Is there specific emphasis on physical appearance for either sex? What are

the expectations of each sex? How do the male and female characters interact with each other (opposite sex)? How do they interact
with others from the same sex? Do you notice any differences in
mannerisms or tone and language use when interacting with the
same or opposite sex? How are heterosexual and same sex couple
represented differently?

Gender is a socially constructed phenomenon. Consequently,
critical literacy of this theme forces students to think about where
gender roles originated and how they are promoted. Have students keep a log of the kind of commercials aired during sporting
events, soap operas, and morning cartoons. Are commercials targeting specific genders? What are the products being advertised?
What messages are being sent to viewers about the product in the
commercial? Explain and describe in the log.

In-Class Discussion: *Changing Values*

How are Young Ju's values changing? How is she adapting a more
American value system? How do her parents deal with her changes? Why do you think they respond this way? Do you have the
same values as your parents or friends? How did you come to
acquiring those new values? What happened when you adopted
values different from others?

> **One Step Further**
> To extend this activity, you can explore the politics of American
> bilingualism. Have students look at the English-only movement
> and debate whether or not America should embrace languages other
> than English. (You can also look at the variety of Western European
> countries that are multilingual and discuss whether or not the debate
> is really about preserving language.)

Part 3: Struggling to be American (pp. 82–143)

In-Class Discussion: *Struggling to Learn English?*

Why do you think Apa feels anxious at the INS offices? Discuss
how immigrants often lack the necessary language skills to comfortably communicate. If you have immigrant students or ELLs in
your class, ask them to share their stories if they feel comfortable.
Despite the millions of immigrants in this country, many government offices are not equipped with multilingual officers or trans-
lations of important documents in foreign languages. Recently in
New York City, Mayor Michael Bloomberg ordered that all government offices make necessary documents (like driver's license
applications, etc.) available in six major languages. With over two
million immigrants in New York City, this law will no doubt be

well received by many. Ask students how they feel about this. Should the United States accommodate ELLs? Why or why not?

In-Class Discussion: *Pressure*

Uhmma insists that Apa was a kinder and gentler man in Korea. Assuming this is true, why do you think Apa changed so radically? How did he devolve from a responsible parent into an abusive adult? Think of Apa's workload and experience as an immigrant. Do you think it could have affected him? Explain.

In-Class Discussion: *Becoming Too American*

What does Apa mean when he accuses Young Ju of being too American? What is he really saying about Young Ju? How have her values, interests, and worldviews changed? Why does this anger Apa? Didn't he come to America willingly, even happily? What do you think is really going on? Have ELLs reflect on their experiences. If you have biracial or multiracial students in your class, pose the following questions: With which culture do you identify? Why? Have you struggled with cultural identity issues? Did you ever feel you didn't belong in one, or both cultural groups? Do people from your home country feel you have "sold out" or lost your cultural identity and have become "too American?" Share your stories or write about it in your journals.

In-Class Discussion: *Choices*

Why does Uhmma believe she has no choices? Do you think Uhmma has a choice? Why does Young Ju believe there is always a choice? Where did she get this belief? Do you believe that a person always has choices? Explain.

Part 4: The American Dream (pp. 144–154)

In-Class Discussion: *American Dreams*

Uhmma tells Young Ju that she is from a family of dreamers. In Young Ju's story, is there a price for dreams? Who pays that price? Reflect on your own life. What are your dreams? Do your parents/ friends support your dreams? Will your dreams come at a price? Explain.

In-Class Discussion: *Scars*

Discuss what Young Ju mean when she says: "I study these lines of history and wish to erase them. Remove the scars, the cuts, fill in the cracks in the skin. I envelop Uhmma's hands in my own tender palms. Close them together. Like a book. A Siamese prayer. I tell her, I wish I could erase these scars for you" (p. 153). Why does Young Ju want to erase the "lines of history," her mother's scars? Have you ever felt like you had to hide a cultural marking or scar? If yes, under what circumstances? Share.

Post-Reading Activity: Heritage Project

This project can be incorporated in an ELA or social studies, computer science, journalism, or library class. This project also provides a great opportunity to talk to students about good research methods. For your convenience, a printable guide for this activity ("Heritage Project") has been provided in the Appendix.

To ground the issue of immigration in relevance, this project encourages your students to explore their own (either personal or family) immigration process. This project will be multidimensional and include pictures, maps, interviews, and video recordings. The project is divided into three stages.

One Step Further

If time permits, watch an episode of *Who Do You Think You Are?* Discuss the research methods the participants used. Have your students outline their own research plans. We encourage you to participate in this project and share your own findings with your students. This is a great way to model this assignment and connect with your students.

Stage 1: *Researching*

The first step in the Heritage Project is research. This includes conducting family interviews and searching various Internet databases like www.ellisisland.org for information. Online sources can be difficult to search, so encourage your students to talk to their relatives. Working in pairs, have your students write good interview questions and try them out on each other.

Stage 2: *Analyzing*

The second step in the Heritage Project is analyzing all the information that's been collected. Students should be able to identify the key themes of their family's narrative. Where did they come from? Why did they leave their native land? Where in the U.S. did they first settle? If students are unable to answer these questions, have them pose further questions. Remember the roadblocks can open more doors and generate greater exploration.

Stage 3: *Reporting*

The final stage in the Heritage Project is reporting the information that's been discovered. This should be done in the form of presentation. Depending on ability and resources, students can create a multimedia report in the form of a poster with pictures and maps, a video with family interviews, or even a blog post on a class website.

Text 2: *The Absolutely True Diary of a Part-Time Indian* by Sherman Alexie

This National Book Award winner explores issues of class and identity through the eyes of an extremely likeable and warm hero.

> ### What Is *The Absolutely True Diary of a Part-Time Indian* About?
>
> Who am I? Where do I come from? At some point or another, we all struggle with identity. *The Absolutely True Diary of a Part-Time Indian* speaks to the reader from the perspective of a nonstereotypical Spokane Indian teen. In this humorous and honest book, students can explore the tensions between past and present, tradition and modernity, and the quest to fulfill personal dreams while belonging to a community.

Lesson Opener: I am . . .

America is a country rich with cultures. This diversity is what gives America its vibrancy, its spice, and its color. To help us make sense of all the people we meet, we tend to categorize individuals into groups. While this helps us understand broad differences between people and distinguish between different traditions, it does make us vulnerable to stereotyping and pigeonholing whole groups of people. In this activity, we use literature to explore this concept. For your convenience, a printable guide for this activity ("I Am . . . Me?") has been provided in the Appendix.

Begin the discussion by asking your students to share their thoughts on the term *cultural diversity*. Explain how, just like your classroom, the world is a rich tapestry of cultures, and the more we learn about people different from ourselves, the more we enrich our own lives. Then, begin discussing the idea of stereotypes. (You can use media images to develop this point.) Explain that stereotypes can be very harmful and prevent us from seeing people as they truly are. To avoid this, we must constantly work to challenge and deconstruct stereotypes and see people for the unique individuals they are.

Though you can use any materials that address these themes, we suggest a culturally rich sample of poems and songs that focus on the struggle to hold onto a unique voice and culture: "Waiting at the Railroad Café" by Janet Wong; "Learning Silence" by Maria Mazziotti Gillan; "Forgotten Language" by Shel Silverstein; "If I a Gay" by R. Zamora Linmark; and "In the Depths of My Solitude" by Tupac Shakur. To do this activity, have your students work through the guide in groups, identifying the author's voice and his or her struggle to escape stereotyping.

One Step Further

After discussing the various perspectives and struggles with identity, students can create their own identity project. Answering the question: "Who Am I?" students can write a poem, a song, or create a poster collage to present to the class. These projects can then be displayed as a gallery for other classes and parents to enjoy.

Pre-Reading Activity: The John Wayne of Spokane

The main character of Sherman Alexie's book, a Spokane freshman, leaves the reservation to attend an all-white school. Caught between two worlds with two very different value systems, Junior struggles to forge his own path in his complicated world. In addition to this struggle, Junior, as a character, challenges the Indian stereotype; he is born with physical disabilities and is allergic to grass. By working against this stereotype, the author not only provides a window into Junior's individual struggle for identity, but questions how we view others and whether we view people with as much complexity as we view ourselves. To elaborate on this point, we suggest teachers address a deeply ingrained stereotype, the Western Myth. For your convenience, a printable guide for this activity ("Debunking the Western Myth") has been provided in the Appendix.

To begin this activity, ask your students what they know about Native Americans. Show your students a clip from an old Western movie, for example, *Stagecoach, Fort Apache, The Last of the Mohicans,* or *Drums Along the Mohawk.* Explore together:

- When was the film made?

- Who created/produced this film?

- Who do you think was the targeted audience of this film?

- How are Native Americans depicted in this film? Why?

- How are non-Native Americans depicted in this film? Why?

- Does this film support or debunk the Western Myth? How?

After discussing the Western Myth and its impact on American culture, show your students a clip from a documentary such as *500 Nations* and revisit the questions. Explain that like the main character in the book, the author of *The Absolutely True Diary of a Part-Time Indian*, Sherman Alexie, is a Spokane Indian. Discuss if and how that changes their view of the book. Encourage your students to document how the author treats the Native American stereotype and Western Myth throughout the text.

Activity: Walking in Someone Else's Shoes

The main character of *The Absolutely True Diary of a Part-Time Indian*, Junior, not only faces cultural isolation as a Spokane Indian, but also as a result of his disabilities. This book provides an important opportunity to discuss the nature of disability and address our perceptions of it. If there are any students in your class that are physically disabled, approach them *before* class and ask if they would be comfortable sharing their personal story. Another suggestion is giving students a chance to experience what it's like to be disabled. Divide students into pairs; designate one student with a "disability" and the other as their "helper." Create a variety of disabilities. Represent the spectrum of disabilities including paralysis, blindness, and hearing impairments. Rent a wheelchair and borrow a set of crutches, blindfold several students, and have others use earplugs. Then, have all the "disabled" students along with their helpers participate in a typical classroom activity. We recommend a P.E. lesson, where students have to play catch or hula hoop. Following the activity, have students switch roles. Afterwards, in small groups, students should reflect on their experience using the following discussion questions:

- Prior to this activity how did you perceive disability?

- What informed your perceptions?

- After completing this activity, how has your perception of the disabled changed? Why?

- How are people with disabilities depicted in the media?

- If you are familiar with the TV show *Glee*, think of the character Artie. Do you think he is an authentic depiction of people with disabilities? Does the fact that the actor playing Artie is not disabled change the authenticity of the character?

Reading Activity: Questions & Discussion Topics

It is very important for lessons to be rooted in the text. According to research, many students lack good textual analytical skills. To address this deficit, critical literacy, which tends to explore generative themes, must also be grounded in real textual examples. To balance these two goals, we have created both reading comprehension questions and in-class discussion topics/activities that include critical textual analysis. To encourage your own growth as an educator, comprehension questions have only been provided for the first chapter. We have also provided discussion topics for the entire text. To save class time, we recommend the questions be done for homework, and class time be used for the in-class discussions and activities. Because of the personal nature of the discussion topics, you may want to consider giving students time to reflect in a reading log or private diary.

Chapter: The Black-Eye-of-the-Month Club (pp. 1–6)

1. Who is the book dedicated to? What does it tell you about the author?

2. What does it mean to have "water on the brain" and "extra brain grease" (p. 2)? What is the narrator's medical condition?

3. What does the narrator reveal in his description of his medical condition?

4. Think of the way the author begins the book. Does it catch your attention? Why or why not?

5. Why did the speaker have so many teeth? How were his teeth removed? What does it tell you about his living conditions?

6. Where does the speaker live? How does he describe the reservation?

7. Describe the speaker's other physical differences.

8. Does the speaker write the way he speaks? What does it tell you about writing?

9. How do other people treat the speaker?

10. What is another way that the author communicates? Why does he draw?

11. Why does the author feel that the only way he can become rich and famous is by becoming an artist? Why is that the only way to get off the rez?

In-Class Discussion: *Lifeboats*

Analyze the phrase: "I think of the world as a series of broken dams and floods, and my cartoons are tiny little lifeboats" (p. 6). How does Junior see his world? How does he cope with his life's difficulties? How do you cope when you are faced with challenges? What is your "lifeboat"?

Chapter: Why Chicken Means So Much to Me (pp. 7–14)

In-Class Discussion: *Dangerous Thinking*

On page 13, Junior tells us: "It sucks to be poor, and it sucks to feel that you somehow *deserve* to be poor. You start believing that you're poor because you're stupid and ugly. And then you start believing that you're stupid and ugly because you're Indian. And because you're Indian you start believing you're destined to be poor. It's an ugly circle and *there's nothing you can do about it*." Do you think Junior really believes that he deserves to be poor? Who does he blame his poverty on? Why is this a dangerous way of thinking? Think about what it means to be poor. How would your life change if you were poor? If you have experienced poverty (in the past or present), do you believe you or your family deserved it? What economic and political conditions create a culture of poverty? How do you perceive poor people? How do you think people from other social classes perceive those living in poverty?

Chapter: Revenge Is My Middle Name (pp. 15–24)

In-Class Discussion: *Rowdy Is Rowdy*

Explore Rowdy's character. What is he like? What is his family like? Why do you think he's named Rowdy? Discuss the title of this chapter. Also, explore other characters' names. What is the author trying to reveal about them? Why do you think Junior has two names?

Chapter: Because Geometry Is Not a Country Somewhere Near France (pp. 25–31)

In-Class Discussion: *State of Tears*

Junior is forced to use his mother's old textbook in school. Why does it make his "hopes and dreams floated up in a mushroom

cloud" (p. 31)? Why does it make him feel like the world has de-
clared nuclear war on him? What does the textbook reveal about
the rez's state of affairs? Who is responsible?

Chapter: Hope against Hope (pp. 32–43)

In-Class Discussion: *Killing Hope*

Why does Mr. P. tell Junior: "If you stay on this rez . . . they're
going to kill you. I'm going to kill you. We're all going to kill you.
You can't fight us forever" (p. 43). What does Mr. P. mean when
he says "kill you"? What would he end up killing inside Junior?
How would the other Indians end up "killing" Junior too? Why
would this happen? Why can't it be stopped?

Chapter: Go Means Go (pp. 44–47)

In-Class Discussion: *Compare & Contrast*

Where is Reardan? What type of school is it? Why is it so extraor-
dinary that Junior wants to go to Reardan? Create a Venn diagram
comparing and contrasting the rez school to Reardan. Are there
schools in your local area that are "different" in physical structure,
student population/demographics, resources, and size? Create a
Venn diagram comparing and contrasting two schools in your
community (or compare to a neighboring community or district).
What accounts for the differences in the two schools? Why such
a difference? How does the community or local and state officials
(politicians) play a role in the quality of schools?

Chapter: Rowdy Sings the Blues (pp. 48–53)

In-Class Discussion: *Changing Times*

Explore Rowdy's reaction to Junior's leaving. Why do you think
he responds in this way? Why does Junior tell us that Rowdy hates
hope? Do you think he does? Have you ever felt like Junior or like
Rowdy? Reflect on this experience in your reading log.

Chapter: How to Fight Monsters (pp. 54–66)

In-Class Discussion: *Winners and Losers*

On his first day of school, Junior's father tells him that the white
kids are no better than he is. But Junior believes that his dad is
wrong, and that his dad is just a "loser Indian father of a loser
Indian son living in a world built for winners" (p. 55). Who are
the winners? Who are the losers? Who designed it to be this way?

Why? Do you agree or disagree with Junior or his father? Does society privilege some over others? How so? How can we change this power dynamic?

On page 61, Junior and Penelope engage in a brief exchange during class about Junior's *real* name and where he is from. Upon learning Junior is from the rez, Penelope pokes fun at the way he speaks by quipping, "That's why you talk so funny." As a result of this comment, Junior "freaks" and doesn't say another word for six days. He is self-conscious of his stutter, lisp, and his "singsong reservation accent." What kind of message is the author sending about dialect (accent) differences? What messages are sent about disability? Whose dialect is validated? How does a comment like the one Penelope makes incite shame and silence? How is this feeling reinforced in society against ELLs, people who speak English but have a dialect or accent, and people who have disabilities? Are there social, political, or educational institutions that promote reactions similar to Penelope's toward speakers who have speech disabilities and/or dialect difference? What can you do to prevent negative reactions against those with learning or physical disabilities?

> ## One Step Further
> After reflecting on Junior's cartoon on page 57, have students create their own self-portraits. What elements comprise their identity? How do they balance different social expectations and cultural associations? Share these works in a class gallery walk and discuss the results.

In-Class Discussion: *Critiquing Cartoons*

On page 60, Junior tells us: "My name is Junior . . . and my name is Arnold. It's Junior and Arnold. I'm both. I felt like two different people inside one body. No, I felt like a magician slicing myself in half, with Junior living on the north side of the Spokane River and Arnold living on the south." With this quote, explore the cartoon on page 57. How does Junior see the differences between White and Indian people? Have students analyze the picture and write down key details that stand out to them. Make sure to analyze the captions, "A BRIGHT FUTURE" on the White side and "A VANISHING PAST" on the Indian side and discuss implications. What are their economic, social, and emotional differences? According to Junior, who created those differences? Why? Do you agree or disagree with his assessment? Explain. Does change in environment necessitate change in cultural or ethnic identity? Why does Junior feel he needs two identities? What do you think influences Junior's feelings of embarrassment towards one side over the other? Who or what influences cultural identity? Who would you rather be—Junior or Arnold? Explain your choice with a partner.

Lesson Activity: Double Vision

Similar to the cartoon on page 57, have students draw their own cartoons choosing various aspects of their cultural heritage that define them. Explain that they don't need to divide their drawings into two neat parts, instead, include all the various influences and connections that make them who they are. Ask them to label these different components, include descriptions explaining how these components reflect them and their unique background. Or, they can draw their own cartoon with a line down the center identifying their culture and another culture they identify with. Write captions around the picture. In their journals, students can write a paragraph explaining why they relate to one side over the other. Post the cartoons around the room as part of a gallery walk.

Chapter: Grandmother Gives Me Some Advice (pp. 67–73)

Analyze the graphic of "My Grandmother" on page 69. What does it tell us about grandma? What do you think of grandma's advice? Would you value her advice? Why or why not? What if the same advice came from another member of the family? Would it have the same affect?

Chapter: Tears of a Clown (pp. 74–76)

In-Class Discussion: *Structuring a Story*

Why do you think the author includes the story of Junior's first love here? Draw out the plot of the novel. What insight does this story give to the rest of the novel?

Chapter: Halloween (pp. 77–81)

In-Class Discussion: *Disguising Love*

Even though he is in love with Penelope, Junior believes he has little hope of impressing her. Why? Rowdy tells him "to change the way you look, the way [you] talk[s], and the way [you] walk" (p. 81). Why? Do you think Junior has to change who he is to be Prince Charming? Have you ever changed aspects of yourself to impress someone? If yes, what changes did you make? What were the changes based on (physical appearance or mannerisms)? If Junior was White and from a wealthy family, do you think he would struggle with his identity? Do you think he would change himself to impress a girl? If Junior was biracial (White and Asian) from a wealthy family, do you think he would change himself to impress a girl? What if the character of Junior was a female? How does a female change herself to impress a boy? How does this change the outcome of the story, if at all? What if the main character of the story was LBTQ? How would this change the outcome of the story, if at all?

Chapter: Slouching toward Thanksgiving (pp. 82–98)

In-Class Discussion: *Knowing That You Don't Know*

In talking to Gordy, Junior experiences a stunning revelation when Gordy says "the world, even the smallest parts of it, is filled with things you don't know." How does this change his view of Wellpinit? How does it help Junior appreciate his own culture more? Did this passage change the way you view the world? How so?

Chapter: My Sister Sends Me an E-mail (pp. 99–100)

In-Class Discussion: *The Grass Is Always Greener*

Is the grass always greener on the other side? Draw a picture based on Mary's description of the Flathead Reservation.

Activity

Show clips of programs broadcast by MTV such as *MTV Cribs*, *My Super Sweet Sixteen*, *The Hills*, *Run's House*, *Jersey Shore*, or *Keeping Up with the Kardashians*. Is the grass always greener on the other side? Explain. Would you trade places with any of the "characters" in these programs? Why or why not? Are the lives and/or material possessions of these "characters" represented in a fair and accurate manner? How do the executive producers, producers, directors, writers, and editors of the program portray the characters? What does MTV have to gain in airing these programs? What advertisements or products are aired during commercials? Examine media ownership and research the corporation that owns MTV. Answer = VIACOM. How much is VIACOM profiting from these programs?

Chapter: Thanksgiving (pp. 101–103)

In-Class Discussion

Why does Junior think it's funny that Native Americans celebrate Thanksgiving? Do you think it's funny? Why or why not? What have you learned in your social studies class about Native Americans and Thanksgiving? How are Native Americans described in your textbooks? What language is used to describe them? Discuss the linguistic bias found in many textbooks that use words like "savages," "roaming," or "wandering" when describing Native Americans. These words implicitly justify the search and seizure of land by White settlers.

Chapter: Hunger Pains (pp. 104–113)

In-Class Discussion: *Pain*

Junior understands pain. His whole life, he has been surrounded by addicts. When he realizes that Penelope "gorges on her pain and then throws it up and flushed it away" (p. 107), how does he react? How does Junior try to help her? How does Penelope respond? Is he successful? Explain. How do social class and poverty factor into the pain Junior experiences and witnesses around him?

In-Class Discussion: *Dreams*

On page 112, Junior tells us: "I couldn't make fun of her for that dream. It was my dream, too. And Indian boys weren't supposed to dream like that. And white girls from small towns weren't supposed to dream big, either. We were supposed to be happy with our limitations. But there was no way Penelope and I were going to sit still. Nope, we both wanted to fly." What dream is Junior referring to? Why are White girls from small towns and Indians not supposed to dream that dream? How are he and Penelope challenging their limitations? How are they overcoming the obstacles they face? Analyze the statement: "Regardless of race, culture, or ethnicity, people from the same social class background experience similar struggles." Is this statement true or false? Defend your answer and give examples.

Chapter: Rowdy Gives Me advice About Love (pp. 114–117)

In-Class Discussion: *Trophies*

What do you think Rowdy means when he tells Junior that he's "sick of Indian guys who treat white women like bowling trophies" (p. 115)? The language of this quote reveals a great deal about the history of Anglo–Indian relations. Since the discovery of North America, Native Americans have been dominated by their White American conquerors. Despite this history of dominance, why do you think an Indian man would want to be with a White woman? Why would she be considered a "bowling trophy"? Also, by referring to her as bowling trophy, what does Rowdy reveal about how Indian men treat White women? What does calling her a "bowling trophy" reveal about her true value? Is this a real "victory"? Do you think a White woman being with an Indian man would also be considered winning a "bowling trophy"? Why or why not?

Chapter: Dance, Dance, Dance (pp. 118–129)

In-Class Discussion: *Poverty*

In your opinion, does Junior struggle more with his Indian identity or his socioeconomic level? Is he more ashamed of being a Native American or being poverty stricken? Are the two linked? Analyze the graphic on page 120. How does Junior socially navigate his poverty? Why?

Chapter: Don't Trust Your Computer (pp. 130–132)

In-Class Discussion: *Changing Colors*

On page 131, Junior tells Gordy that "Some Indians think you *become* white if you try to make your life better, if you become successful." What does it mean to become "white"? Consider mannerisms, dress, style, walk, and language—the way you talk and sound—as you contemplate your answer. Why do Indians (or any other social group) feel betrayed if you try to improve your life outside of the social constrictions? Is there any way to deal with this kind of situation? Explain. What does Gordy mean when he says "life is a constant struggle between being an individual and being a member of the community" (p. 132)?

Chapter: My Sister Sends Me a Letter (pp. 133–134)

In-Class Discussion: *Is Romance Dead?*

What is the title of Mary's life story? Do you think it's an appropriate title? Why or why not? Do you think Mary's notion of romance has changed? Why?

Chapter: Reindeer Games (pp. 135–149)

In-Class Discussion: *Getting Committed*

What does Coach mean when he says, "The quality of a man's life is in direct proportion to his commitment to excellence, regardless of his chosen field of endeavor" (p. 148)? Why do you think Junior is so committed? What do you think he's so committed to?

Chapter: And a Partridge in a Pear Tree (pp. 150–151)

In-Class Discussion: *Holiday Cheer?*

What are the holidays like at Junior's house? What does Junior's father do at Christmas? Why do you think he does this? How does Junior really feel about his father's behavior? What does Junior get for Christmas? Why does it mean so much to him? Why is the five-dollar bill a "beautiful and ugly thing"?

Chapter: Red Versus White (pp. 152–158)

In-Class Discussion: *Forgiveness, Love, and Tolerance*

In this chapter, Junior loses someone very dear to him. From this experience, he begins to recognize and appreciate his own Indian traditions and beliefs. In the old days, how were eclectic people viewed by their fellow Indians? How did Indians lose their tradition of tolerance? How is this notion of tolerance reflected in grandmother? How does the chapter title emphasize this?

Chapter: Wake (pp. 159–167)

In-Class Discussion: *Grandmother Spirit*

Who is Ted? Why does he come to the wake? Though Ted claims to feel Indian, is he? Why or why not? This episode deeply affects the community; it unifies them and leads Junior to say "each funeral was a funeral for all of us." Why do you think that is? Does this spirit of unity last? What does he mean when Junior says, "And all of us laughed as we walked and drove and rode our way back to our lonely, lonely, houses" (p. 167)?

Chapter: Valentine Heart (pp. 168–178)

In-Class Discussion: *A World of People Who Are Not Assholes*

Responding to his teacher's horrible remark, Junior says, "I used to think the world was broken down by the tribes . . . by black and white. By Indian and white. But I know that isn't true. The world is only broken into two tribes: The people who are assholes and the people who are not" (p. 176). How has Junior's view of White people changed? What does he come to realize about the world? Do you feel society is broken down into "tribes"? If yes, how so? Which "tribe" do you belong to? Who makes up these "tribes"? How does one become a member of a "tribe"? Does race (or class, gender, sexuality) play a role in belonging to a group, or "tribe"? Do we live in a color-blind society where attitudes and behaviors play a more important role than racial identity? Explain.

Chapter: In Like a Lion (pp. 179–196)

In-Class Discussion: *The Battle Within*

Study the graphic on page 182; what is Junior struggling with? Why does he feel like "one of those Indian scouts who led the U.S. Cavalry against other Indians" (p. 182)?

In-Class Discussion: *The Game of Life*

Why has basketball made Junior feel like he's "grow[n] up really fast, too fast" (p. 184)? How has it made him see "that every choice [he] make[s] is important . . . and that a basketball game, even a game between two small schools in the middle of nowhere, can be the difference between being happy and being miserable for the rest of [his] life" (p. 184)?

Chapters: Rowdy and I Have a Long and Serious Discussion about Basketball & Because Russian Guys Are Not Always Geniuses (pp. 197–214)

In-Class Discussion: *Guilt*

How does Junior and Rowdy's relationship change? Why does it begin to change? Why does Junior feel that his sister "burned to death because [he] had decided that [he] wanted to spend [his] life with white people" (p. 211)? How does Junior cope with all his guilt? Do you experience guilt? How do you cope with it?

Chapter: Remembering (pp. 215–218)

In-Class Discussion: *The Tribe of Tribes*

At his family's graves, Junior has a life-changing realization. He realizes that although he is a Spokane Indian belonging to that tribe, he belongs to many other tribes as well. What are some of the other tribes Junior belongs to? Why is this realization so significant? Why does Junior suddenly know that everything is going to be okay? What tribes do you belong to? How can we learn to start focusing more on the things we have in common? How can we unite to change the things we all struggle with (economic, social, and political action)?

Chapter: Talking about Turtles (pp. 219–230)

In-Class Discussion: *Growing Up*

How does the story conclude? How does Junior and Rowdy's friendship change? What do you think Junior means when he says, "I hoped and prayed that they would someday forgive me for leaving them. I hoped and prayed that I would someday forgive myself for leaving them" (p. 230)? Is this what growing up is all about (to eventually leave your community)? Does leaving your community mean you are abandoning your cultural values and/or identity? Explain. What does this quote mean to you?

Post-Reading Activity: The Arrival

> This activity begins with a whole-class reading of Shaun Tan's brilliant book, *The Arrival*. In this text, several immigration stories are told without the use of print. You may want to consider having your students present their Heritage Projects here, at the conclusion of the unit.

Step 1: *Before Reading*

> As the saying goes, a picture is worth a thousand words. Before beginning the book, discuss with students how we "read" pictures. Explore what clues we look for to understand the stories behind the images. What are the benefits and consequences of creating a book without text?

Step 2: *Reading*

> As you read *The Arrival*, you will notice that the text is divided into five general sections. They represent the five phases of the arrival's travels: leaving, journeying, arriving, acclimating, and localizing. You will also notice that while Tan's drawings seem vaguely reminiscent of Ellis Island, they are not of New York. Additionally, any print in the book is not readable. This is done in order to give readers the experience of the arrival.

Step 3: *After Reading*

> Who are you? Where do you come from? What experiences have shaped the person you are today? Have each student create a collage, short film, song, spoken-word poetry, graphic novel, or an essay exploring his/her own family journeys. These presentations can be shared with the class.

CHAPTER SIX

Gender Wars

Persepolis at the House on Mango Street

"The boys and the girls live in separate worlds."
—Esperanza in *The House on Mango Street* (Cisneros, 1991, p. 8)

Education makes sense because women and men learn that through learning they can make and remake themselves, because women and men are able to take responsibility for themselves as beings capable of knowing—of knowing that they know and knowing that they don't. (Freire, 2004, p. 15)

Why Talk about Gender?

If I were a boy . . . " sings Beyoncé. If I were a boy, would my life be different? Definitely. From a very young age, we are all conditioned to think of men and women in different ways. While the specific expectations vary by society, we are all cast into particular gender roles without even realizing it. Though these roles are socially constructed and constantly evolving, they continue to define, encourage, and limit us in different ways.

There has been much recent buzz on the issue of gender. In Egypt, women played a major role in the country's recent revolution and its emerging democracy. Domestically, "Don't Ask, Don't Tell," a policy forbidding openly gay servicemen and women from serving in the armed forces, has been repealed, calling into question how Americans view gender in these roles. Despite these strides, women, who outnumber men on most college campuses, are still discriminated in the workplace, earning on average only 75 percent of what their male co-workers do (White House Council on Women and Girls, 2011).

Critical literacy argues that we are all deeply influenced by the social structures we are embedded in. This means that the neighborhoods we grow up in, the friends we surround ourselves with, the communities we are immersed in, all inform and shape who we are. Whether explicit or not, these social spheres are rooted in value systems. They not only privilege certain groups over others, but mold and purport specific gender roles.

Educators should never limit their students. Teachers must always be conscious of not encouraging restrictive gender roles like "girls are bad at math" and "boys hate reading." Instead, teachers should reflect on their practice and engage in frequent discussions with their students, guiding them to address how gender roles are constructed and the role gender plays in their own lives.

To begin the conversation, this unit centers on three very different pieces of literature, each of which brings a unique voice and perspective to the issue of gender. Sandra Cisneros' *The House on Mango Street* has a very local feel; the forces shaping Esperanza's life are clear and direct. In contrast, Marjane Satrapi's *Persepolis: The Story of a Childhood* has a global feel; Marji is influenced by a bevy of Western pop culture, Eastern traditions, and eclectic individuals. In the final text, Peter Sis' *The Wall: Growing Up Behind the Iron Curtain*, the author visually explores how the arts influenced and shaped his life as a young man growing up in communist Czechoslovakia.

How Do I Use This Unit?

In this unit, we explore the role of gender, primarily through the eyes of two very different young women. In *The House on Mango Street*, Esperanza is a Chicago-born Latina, struggling to determine her own future. In *Persepolis,* an autobiographical work, Marji is an Iranian girl struggling to find herself amid the brutality of the Islamic Revolution. We conclude the unit with a classroom reading of *The Wall: Growing Up Behind the Iron Curtain*, an illustrated autobiography describing the author's childhood in communist Czechoslovakia.

Because two of the focus texts are told from the female perspective, it is very important to keep your male students' involved. We recommend having your students periodically consider the story from a male perspective. You can even ask them to write a parallel story of one of the male characters.

Because of its setting, many urban schools seem to have *The House on Mango Street* on their reading short list. If you live in a suburban or rural area, we still highly recommend this text for a number of reasons. First, its very short chapters make it an interesting book for all students, especially those who are struggling or typically disinterested in reading. Second, even though it's set in a big city, it has a very small-town feel. In contrast, *Persepolis* is set in a variety of exotic locations; Marji lives in Iran, attends school in Europe, and is obsessed with Western pop culture. For these reasons, it tends to appeal to a wide range of students and is a great read for any teenager.

In this unit, we not only provide a multitude of perspectives, but tap into very different forms of media. In doing so, we hope to expand your students' notion of text and introduce them to a new variety of school-worthy materials. *The House on Mango Street* is uniquely structured with short focused chapters and is most commonly used for language-arts or reading classes. *Persepolis*, a multifaceted award-winning graphic novel, is hardly taught in schools, but can easily be incorporated into a modern history lesson, cultural studies section, or literature unit. Like *The House on Mango Street*, *Persepolis* has very short chapters and reads very quickly. *The Wall*, a Caldecott Honor book, presents as an oversized children's book, providing textual layers that will help your students develop visual literacy skills in a short, easily read text.

Text 1: *The House on Mango Street* by Sandra Cisneros

The House on Mango Street is a common secondary school text. It's a modern coming-of-age novel that speaks to adolescents of all walks of life, even those who didn't grow up on Mango Street.

> ### What Is *The House on Mango Street* About?
> Told in a series of vignettes, *The House on Mango Street* offers the reader snapshots of life in a Chicano and Puerto Rican–American Chicago neighborhood. The stories, told by a young girl named Esperanza, explore the various characters who live in her community and the important events that shape how she views herself and the world.

Lesson Opener: Location, Location, Location

Because Esperanza's neighborhood plays a major role in how she views both herself and the world, it is important to open this unit by exploring the impact of space in our lives. For this activity, we recommend reading two short stories, set in two very different places, and exploring how each affects both the story and the characters. A printable guide for this activity ("Location, Location, Location") has been provided in the Appendix. This activity can also be completed by using the "Power Walk" printable guide previously used in the unit on *Push*.

If you have a reading textbook, we recommend perusing the collection for a story that focuses on setting. Many readers have short stories or novellas that specifically focus on this topic. If you do not have such a text, we recommend any story from the collection *Big City Cool: Short Stories about Urban Youth* (Weiss & Weiss, 2002). These stories are all set in an urban cityscape. To contrast this, we recommend that the second story be set in a rural area, for example, *The Lottery* by Shirley Jackson.

Divide your students in groups to read the stories together. If time is especially limited, have the students read the texts at home. Then, in groups, have them work through the guide together. Review the material together by engaging in a class discussion about the role that setting plays in both stories. Then, in a reading journal or creative writing assignment, students can reflect on the following questions:

- Where do you live?

- What is your neighborhood like?

- Who lives in your neighborhood? Describe the demographics.

- Describe the homes, stores, restaurants, or other community organizations present in your neighborhood (if any).

- What do you like and dislike about your neighborhood?

- If you could change any aspect of your neighborhood, what would it be?

- How does where you live affect the person you are?

Pre-Reading Activity: Chapters of My Life

The House on Mango Street is uniquely structured; it's a series of short vignettes or "mini-stories," each highlighting an important moment, object, or individual in Esperanza's life. For your convenience, a printable guide for this activity ("The Chapters of My Life") has been provided in the Appendix.

One Step Further

Students can then write, publish, and exchange their table of contents. (If appropriate, this can be done anonymously.) Each student should have an opportunity to read another student's work. Then, in a writing assignment, they can try to interpret that person's life story by writing text for a book flap or back cover.

Have your class read through the table of contents of *The House on Mango Street*. Explain that each title represents a brief encounter, a moment in time that somehow powerfully impacted Esperanza's life. Together, read through the chapter titles and try to brainstorm what those brief moments may have been about. Next, skim through the pages of the entire book. Examine the pages focusing specifically on dialect and language use. Are there any words or phrases that are unfamiliar to you? Are there any words written in non-standard form? If yes, what do you think the author's intent was when including such words, phrases, or dialect? Which groups come to mind when you see (and imagine hearing) this dialect?

After the students get a feel for this, ask them to imagine that they are writing a book with this structure. As Esperanza's story was about her life, their books will be about their lives. Using the guide provided in the Appendix, ask them to write their own chapter titles, making sure to include all the important moments, people, and events that shaped who they are today.

Reading Activities: Questions & Discussion Topics

It is very important for lessons to be rooted in the text. According to research, many students lack good textual analytical skills. To address this deficit, critical literacy, which tends to explore generative themes, must also be grounded in real textual examples. To balance these two goals, we have created both reading comprehension questions and in-class discussion topics/activities that include critical textual analysis. To encourage your own growth as an educator, comprehension questions have been provided only for the first part of the book. We have also provided discussion topics for the entire text. To save class time, we recommend the questions be done for homework, and class time be used for the in-class discussions and activities. To provide a sense of continuity and focus to the chapters, we have divided the book into several parts.

Part 1: Self-Definition & Identity (pp. 3–11)

Chapter: *The House on Mango Street*

1. What does this chapter tell us about Esperanza?

2. Why did Esperanza's family have to leave the flat on Loomis?

3. What was Esperanza expecting in her new house?

4. Does Esperanza like Mango Street? Why or why not?

5. Why do you think the nun was surprised when she heard where Esperanza lived?

Chapter: *Hairs*

1. How does Esperanza describe her family?

2. From the information provided in the vignette, what do you think her family life is like?

> ### One Step Further
> As a writing or drawing assignment, have your students focus on one feature of their family (like Esperanza does with hair) and use it to describe what makes them similar and different from their siblings or parents.

Chapter: *Boys & Girls*

1. What does Esperanza mean when she says "the boys and the girls live in separate worlds" (p. 8)? Do you think this is true? Explain.

2. Why is it hard for Esperanza to make new friends?

3. What does Esperanza mean when she says "until then I am a red balloon, a balloon tied to an anchor" (p. 9)? What does this image tell us about Esperanza? Who is the anchor? Is it a good thing or bad thing? Explain.

Chapter: *My Name*

1. Why does Esperanza's name mean different things to different people?

2. Who is Esperanza named after? How does she relate to this person?

3. Why do you think Esperanza wants to rename herself? Why does she feel that "Esperanza" does not reflect who she really is?

4. Do you have different names (like nicknames) that mean different things to different people? Explain.

In-Class Discussion: *Self-Definition and Identity*

How does Esperanza define herself? What is her background? Does her background shape her identity? Explain. How do you describe yourself? How would others describe you? What shapes your identity? How much influence do outside factors, beyond family, culture, and language, have on shaping your identity? Explain.

Part 2: Friendship, Neighborhood, & Home (pp. 12–25)

In-Class Discussion: *"It takes a village to raise a child."*

Describe the various people of the "village" that are a part of Esperanza's life. Pick your favorite character and describe how he or she "raises" and influences Esperanza? Pick a character from your own life and describe how he or she "raises" and influences you.

Part 3: Freedom & Entrapment (pp. 26–38)

In-Class Discussion: *Freedom & Entrapment*

Who on Mango Street is freed? Who is trapped? Why? What do you think the author is trying to say about society? Do you agree with her opinions? Why or why not? Describe a moment in your own life when you felt freed or trapped. How did you react to that feeling? Did it affect the person you are today? Now let's consider social, economic, political, and language factors that could make a person feel freed or trapped. In small groups, give examples of how each category could free you or trap you.

For example, think about language, or the way you speak and/ or sound. How do you think others perceive you when you speak? Do you speak "differently" when you are with your friends? How about if you are speaking to your teacher, principal, or other authority figure, like your boss (if you work part-time or over the summer)? Do you feel judgment is being made about you solely due to how you speak? If so, how can the way you speak either free or trap you from progressing? Do people judging you have to change their perceptions of how you speak, or do you have to change the way you speak to accommodate them?

Part 4: Growth, Maturity, & Sexuality (pp. 39–55)

In-Class Discussion: *Growth, Maturity, and Sexuality*

In this section, how has Esperanza matured emotionally, physically, and sexually? How has growing up on Mango Street shaped the person she is? What neighborhood do you live in? How has it shaped you as you become an adult?

One Step Further

Together read the article "The 9/11 Disappeareds" (Louie, 2001). What is an illegal immigrant? In the case of 9/11, were the families of illegal immigrants able to track their loved ones? How? What sort of community organizations has been set up to help this population? Why are these organizations so important? What is the current government's opinion of illegal immigrants? What do you think? Should millions of illegal immigrants in the USA be granted some form of citizenship? Explain.

Part 5: Gender Roles & Expectations (pp. 56–73)

In-Class Discussion: *Gender Roles & Expectations*

Throughout *The House on Mango Street*, we see different men and women filling specific gender roles. What types of attitudes seem to be held by women? What types of attitudes seem to be held by men? How do the women on Mango Street tend to act? Why do they act this way? Describe the gender roles on Mango Street. What do you think the community expects of women and men? How clearly differentiated are the roles of men and women? Is there any crossover? Why or why not?

Think about your own life. Are there specific expectations from your school, family, or friends because you are a boy/girl? Explain. Choose one group of people and write down a list of their expectations for you. Then, imagine yourself the opposite gender. Write a brief list of what you imagine their new expectations for you would be. Compare the two. Is there any differentiation? Why? What gender roles does society create for us? How are the expectations different for men and women? What happens when people challenge their gender roles (e.g., a gay male or female CEO)? Do you agree with the set gender roles or not? You may also consider including replacing "male" or "female" with LGBT populations to avoid the trap of limiting the analysis to only the socially constructed genders of male and female.

Part 6: Fitting In (pp. 74–87)

In-Class Discussion: *Fitting In*

Does Esperanza manage to fit in somewhere in the social landscape around her, and if so, where? In this section, we are presented with a number of case studies of different people on Mango Street. Does Sally fit in? Do Minerva, Rafaela, and Mamacita? Why or why not? Why do you think these vignettes are included with "Four Skinny Trees" and "Bums in the Attic"? Do they "fit in" with the rest of the narrative? Think about your own life. Do you fit in easily with others? Why or why not? Do you know anyone who does not easily fit in? Why or why not? Is it important to fit in? Give examples of when it's not important to fit in.

Part 7: Future Opportunities & Limitations (pp. 88–102)

In-Class Discussion: *Future Opportunities and Home*

What kinds of opportunities are available to Esperanza and the other girls on Mango Street? Do you feel that Esperanza's mother had genuine opportunities? Does Esperanza? Each episode featured in this section tells us about another opportunity that was made available to Esperanza. Go through the events, are these really opportunities? Explain. How do you think Esperanza sees her future? How does she challenge the future awaiting her?

One Step Further

Where do you think Esperanza will find her home? Why? Do you think the home Esperanza is looking for is a physical home? What does "home" mean to you? Have you found your "home" yet? What do you imagine it looking like? How will you find it? In your reading diary, draw a picture or write a description of your home.

Part 8: Finding Home (pp. 103–110)

In-Class Discussion: *Remember Where You Come From*

After the three sisters tell Esperanza that she will one day leave Mango Street, they add, "You can't erase what you know. You can't forget who you are" (p. 105). What do they mean? Is it possible to forget who you are and where you come from? Why or why not? Why is it important not to forget your past? Is forgetting your past the same thing as "forgetting who you are"?

Post-Reading Activity: The Venturing Muse

Following the theme of the book, this activity encourages students to see their own neighborhood as a source of inspiration, reflection, and personal growth. Additionally, it explores the issue of gender in a familiar and personal way. For your convenience, a printable guide for this activity ("Take a Tour of My Neighborhood") has been provided in the Appendix.

For this activity have your students take a tour of their neighborhood. Using a camera or a video camera (flip cameras are great for this), have your students create a photo-journal essay or documentary of their neighborhood. To help students focus their project, read together John Gay's *The Art of Walking the Streets of*

London. In groups, using highlighter pens in two different colors, have students identify all the men and women the poem's narrator meets walking through the city streets. Following Gay's example, have your students focus their projects on the important men and women in their neighborhood. After the project is complete, students can share their work either in a gallery walk or by publishing a local travel guide.

Text 2: *The Complete Persepolis* by Marjane Satrapi

Like all graphic novels, *Persepolis* can be explored from a variety of angles. Here, we try to focus specifically on Marji's experience as a young woman growing up amid a turbulent time. Despite this particular lens, we urge you to use the graphics, not only as a layer of interpretation, but to build your students' visual literacy skills. Additionally, we have found that among the few schools that read this text, most only read Part 1. If possible, we highly recommend reading both works with your students as it provides an in-depth and long-range view of Marji's life. A quick note about reading graphic novels. Do not assume that your students will be able to read this text proficiently. Many will initially read either the words or pictures, which will prevent them from grasping the full narrative weight of the text. To avoid this, prepare reading activities that scaffold them throughout this process and guide them in reading both modes simultaneously. We recommend giving students time in class to read independently and then having them work in groups to discuss what they have read. We have found that this structure supports students in their meaning-making process while allowing them to read at their own pace.

> ### What Is *Persepolis* About?
>
> Marjane Satrapi's autobiographical work, *Persepolis*, tells the story of a young girl growing up during the Islamic Revolution. The book follows Marji through a tumultuous childhood, adolescence, and adulthood. Told in cinematographic black-and-white elegance, Satrapi captures a young woman's maturation amid a troubling historical period.

Lesson Opener: It's a Hard Thing Growing Up

Persepolis gives the reader an intimate view of war and a firsthand account of its devastating effects. To help begin this difficult discussion, we recommend studying some of the literature written during or about war. For your convenience, a printable guide for this activity ("It's a Hard Thing Growing Up") has been provided in the Appendix.

Divide your students into groups. Distribute to each group a packet of three war poems. Try to provide poems from a range

> ### One Step Further
> Have your students imagine that they are one of the poets writing in a time of conflict. Have them switch genres by writing two personal journal entries describing the historical events unfolding around them.

of wars and different perspectives. Some poems can focus on actual combat while others can reflect on the struggles to maintain/construct an identity in times of crisis. We recommend: "I Write Hebrew" by Salman Masalha; "Painful Birds" by Elisha Porat; "A Wartime Education" by U. A. Fanthorpe; "Green Beret" by Ho Thein; "Doodlebugs" by Grace Griffiths; "Glory of Women" by Siegfried Sassoon; "Holocaust" by Barbara Sonek.

After the students read their poems, have them respond to the questions in the guide. Together, discuss the issues raised in the different poems, focusing on why it is difficult to grow up during war.

Pre-Reading Activity: KWL, Middle East Edition

To shift the focus to *Persepolis*, activate students' prior knowledge about the situation in the Middle East, specifically the treatment of women in these countries. With most history curricula never quite making it past the Cold War, there is a strong chance that your students have never learned about the Islamic Revolution. This is a wonderful opportunity to teach your students an important chapter of modern history. For your convenience, a printable guide for this activity ("KWL, Middle East Edition") has been provided in the Appendix.

To get your students thinking about the Middle East, divide them into groups and ask them to fill out a K-W-L chart (provided in the Appendix). You can use the graph in a variety of ways, for example you can focus on the role of religion, women's rights, and government. After reviewing what students know (the K column) and what students want to know (the W column), have each group explore one of the topics in the chart. This can be

> ### One Step Further
> If you are reading *Persepolis* as part of a social studies class, explore this topic further, specifically America's involvement in Iran, by reading a chapter from *A People's History of the United States* by historian Howard Zinn. In this graphic adaptation of his bestselling book, Zinn provides a behind-the-scenes view, including America's economic interest in the region, the CIA's role in removing democratic Prime Minister Dr. Mohammad Mossadegh ("Operation Ajax"), and America's involvement in the Islamic Revolution.

done using Internet sources, newspaper articles, or encyclopedias. After each group presents their work, students can fill out what they have learned (the L column). Have your students refer to their graphs throughout reading *Persepolis*.

Reading Activity: Questions & In-class Discussions

It is very important for lessons to be rooted in the text. According to research, many students lack good textual analytical skills. To address this deficit, critical literacy, which tends to explore generative themes, must also be grounded in real textual examples. To balance these two goals, we have created both reading comprehension questions and in-class discussion topics/activities that include critical textual analysis. To encourage your own growth as an educator, comprehension questions have only been provided for the first part of the book. We have also provided discussion topics for the entire text. To save class time, we recommend the questions be done for homework, and class time be used for the in-class discussions and activities. To provide a sense of continuity and focus to the chapters, we have divided the book into several parts.

Part 1: Growing Up in Iran (pp. 3–153)

Chapter: The Veil (pp. 3–9)

1. How old is Marji at the time of the Revolution?

2. Can you see Marji in her class picture? What do you think the author is foreshadowing?

3. How are Marji and her classmates adjusting to the new rule of the Revolution? Do they like them? Explain.

4. How has Marji's world been affected by the Revolution?

5. What are Marji's parents' political leanings? How do they influence her own?

6. Why is everyone so fearful when Mrs. Satrapi's picture was taken during a protest?

7. What does Marji want to be when she grows up? Why? Are you surprised by this? Explain.

8. On page 8, how is God depicted? Why do you think the author did that?

9. Compare how Marji's parents, teacher, and God react when Marji shares what she wants to be when she grows up.

Chapter: The Bicycle (pp. 10–17)

In-Class Discussion: *Class Struggles*

In a nutshell, Marx's theory of dialectical materialism is the belief that "the history of all hitherto existing society is the history of class struggles." (*The Communist Manifesto*, 1848). Marxists believe that human history is made up of the class struggles in our society; as groups attain and lose materialism (status), they revolt, causing history to happen. Do you know of any examples of social classes revolting against ruling powers? Do you think our society is made up of social classes? What defines a social class? Is it possible to leave a social class and join a new one?

Chapter: The Water Cell (pp. 18–25)

In-Class Discussion: *Teaching the Truth*

Even though it is not factual, Marji is taught to believe that the Shah was given his power by God. Why would her school teach her this? What should schools teach? Why? Can there be differences in opinion on this? Why or why not? Consider the controversial debate about teaching evolutionary theory versus intelligent design in schools. What's your opinion on this issue?

Chapter: Persepolis (pp. 26–32)

In-Class Discussion: *Documenting Government-sanctioned Horrors*

Why do you think the government has forbidden people from taking pictures of the revolution? Why would the government not want the outside world to know how they are treating their people? Why would Marji's father risk his life to take pictures? Can you think of any other time in history when a government tried to stop the outside world from knowing the horrors they were committing? Did other countries eventually find out? How? What happened when they did?

Chapter: The Letter (pp. 33–39)

In-Class Discussion: *A Love That Cannot Be*

Analyze the Mehri-Hossein love story. Why do you think Marji's father intervenes? Are you surprised by Hossein's reaction? Why or why not? What does Marji mean when she says, "We were not in the same social class, but at least we were in the same bed" (p. 37).

> **One Step Further**
> To explore this chapter further, debate the current issue involving the torture of Abu Ghraib prisoners. Divide the class into three groups, one representing the prisoners, one the military, and one the Supreme Court justices. After each party presents their argument, supported by valid information, have the "justices" vote whether the government is guilty of torture. Discuss the verdict.

Chapter: The Party (pp. 40–46)

In-Class Discussion: *Sins of the Father*

What does Marji mean when she says, "the battle was over for our parents, but not for us" (p. 44). How do the children continue to fight the war? What is the author alluding to about the nature of children and their involvement in adult affairs?

Chapter: The Heroes (pp. 47–53)

In-Class Discussion: *The Geneva Convention*

The Iranian prisoners were brutally tortured. In class, examine the Geneva Convention. When was the Geneva Convention written? Why was it written? Have all countries adhered to the Convention rules? If no, why do you think they have not?

Chapter: Moscow (pp. 54–61)

In-Class Discussion: *The Path of Our Fathers*

Analyze the final graphic on page 61. How does the author illustrate Marji's feelings after hearing her uncle's story?

Chapter: The Sheep (pp. 62–71)

In-Class Discussion: *Inaccurate Reporting*

Mr. Satrapi never trusts what he watches on Iranian TV. Why? Where does Mr. Satrapi get his news? Why do you think the Iranian news would report inaccuracies? This is not the only time in history when a country deliberately reported incorrect news on their airwaves. Why is it so important to get your information from valid news sources? What makes a news source valid and trustworthy? From what source do you get your news? Are there news sources you do not trust? Name them and explain why you do not trust them.

Activity: *Reporting on Reporters*

This is a great opportunity for students to apply critical thinking. Have your students work in pairs and select a popular news story. Explain that they will be reporting on the reporting. This means they will be exploring different ideologies embedded within different perspectives. Begin by having students collect multiple articles or other media sources on the same story/topic. In New York City, students can buy the *New York Times*, the *New York Post*, and the *New York Daily News*, and read local blogs like Gawker.com or listen to a podcast from WNYC.org. With a partner, students should compare and contrast how each media source tells the story. Who is the audience that each paper targets? What kind of language is used in each paper? (The *Post* and the *Daily News* are both known for intentionally using large, colorful, bold fonts, with words intentionally spelled incorrectly and phonetically, like "prez" for president, and "sez" for says.) Are the reporters truly being objective, or do personal beliefs, values, or professional obligations (political ideologies of the newspaper/corporate beliefs) enter into the reporting in implicit ways? Have students present their findings to the class, naming the perspective or ideology of the newspaper. Have them explain how ideology drives why a story is presented in a particular manner.

Another excellent activity to draw out ideological agendas of newspapers is to buy two or three local newspapers published on the same date to critically analyze use of space, size of print, language used, color versus black-and-white photographs, and coverage and presentation of similar stories. Lay each newspaper side by side and ask: Which stories make the front page, or the first few pages? If each newspaper prints the same story, how does each present the events of the story? How is the main person characterized or described in the article? How can one event be written in multiple ways? Does it change the outcome or perception of the events in the story depending on who writes it or how it is presented?

Chapter: The Trip (pp. 72–79)

In-Class Discussion: *Wearing Ideology*

Even though the government strongly monitored the dress of the people, Marji tells us that the way the clothes were worn quickly became ideological. How can clothes reflect ideology? Do your clothes reflect an ideology; if so, how? Can you think of other times that people have worn or were forced to wear clothes to make a political statement? Who enforces the clothing style? Why? For what purpose?

Chapter: The F-14s (pp. 80–86)

 In-Class Discussion: *O' Say Can You See . . .*

  Discuss the deal the pilots made with the Iranian government. Why do you think they made this deal? Why do you think it moved Marji and her family so much? Discuss "The Star-Spangled Banner," America's national anthem. What does it symbolize? When was it written? When is it sung? Explore the feelings it invokes in you and others. Is it symbolic to participate in the singing of the national anthem? Explain. What does it mean if someone chooses not to sing it? Use the "Critical Literacy/Critical Textual Analysis" printable guide (at the end of the Appendix) to answer additional questions about the national anthem.

Chapter: The Jewels (pp. 87–93)

 In-Class Discussion: *The Jewels*

  Explore the title of the chapter. What do you think "the jewels" are? Provide evidence to support your opinion.

Chapter: The Key (pp. 94–102)

 In-Class Discussion: *The Key to Heaven*

  Why do you think this chapter is called "the key"? Who has been given a key? What does the key symbolize? Why would the government tell this to young men? Does it work? Which group of men does the government specifically want to attract? Why? Is the government's campaign successful? Compare the graphics on page 102; both depict young people in motion. How does the author contrast the realities and lifestyle of these two groups of people? What does it tell us?

Chapter: The Wine (pp. 103–110)

 In-Discussion: *Buying Off the Believers*

  Explore the story of the wine. What do Marji and grandmother do with the wine? What does Marji's father mean when he says, "their faith has nothing to do with ideology! A few bills were all he needed to forget the whole thing!" (p. 110). Why do you think Mr. Satrapi is so angry about this?

Chapter: The Cigarette (pp. 111–117)

 In-Class Discussion: *War & Society*

  Look at the image on the last frame of page 115. Why is this image so evocative? What does it mean to "die a martyr is to inject blood into the veins of society" (p. 115)? Do you agree or disagree? Why?

One Step Further
To explore this chapter further, debate some of the items the U.S. government has historically banned, such as Cuban cigars.

Chapter: The Passport (pp. 118–125)

In-Class Discussion: *A Passport to Freedom*

Explore the difficulties Uncle Taher experiences in trying to obtain a passport. Why do you think the government doesn't readily offer Uncle Taher a passport? What happens to the forger? What is the irony in this story?

Chapter: Kim Wilde (pp. 126–134)

In-Class Discussion: *Social Control*

Why do you think the leaders of the Revolution ban all forms of Western life? Why do they want to control the lives of their people? Should governments be allowed to ban certain things? Why or why not? Does our government ban anything? Give examples and explain the purpose of the ban. Is it fair? Is it a form of control? Or protection?

Chapter: The Shabbat (pp. 135–142)

In-Class Discussion: *A Picture Is Worth a Thousand Words*

Analyze the last frame of the chapter. How does the author convey Marji's emotions?

Chapter: The Dowry (pp. 143–153)

In-Class Discussion: *Escaping Iran*

What causes Marji's parents to decide to send her to a school in Vienna? What are they worried about? Reflect on the Satrapi family's mental state as Marji leaves Iran.

Part 2: Life in Vienna (pp. 155–245)

Chapter: The Soup (pp. 155–163)

In–Class Discussion: *The War after the War*

How does the war continue to affect the lives of people even after they've escaped it? How has the war affected Houshang and Zozo's marriage? Is Shirin aware of the war at all? Do you think she understands her parents' struggles? Why or why not? Does the war continue to affect Marji? How?

Chapter: Tyrol (pp. 164–172)

In-Class Discussion: *Culture Shock*

Compare Marji's interactions with her new school friends to how she acts with Lucia's family. Why is she more apprehensive in Tyrol? What does she learn from both groups of people?

Chapter: Pasta (pp. 173–179)

In-Class Discussion: *Tolerance*

What does Marji mean when she says, "in every religion, you find the same extremists" (p. 178)? What do you think of this phrase? Do you believe it's true? Why or why not?

Chapter: The Pill (pp. 180–188)

In-Class Discussion: *Sexual Freedom*

Why is Marji surprised to learn that her friend is on birth control? After observing her friends' lifestyles, how does Marji feel about sexual freedom? How does she visually express this? Do you share her view? Why or why not?

Chapter: The Vegetable (pp. 189–197)

In-Class Discussion: *Momo vs. Marji*

How does Momo view ordinary people (whom he calls "peons")? According to Momo, what is life about? What is government about? Why does Marji challenge him? What do you think Momo's background is? How does it inform his opinions? Compare and contrast it to Marji's background. How has her experience molded her beliefs? How do they deal with their disagreements?

In-Class Discussion: *The Trouble with Fitting In*

Analyze the phrase, "The harder I tried to assimilate, the more I had the feeling that I was distancing myself from my culture, betraying my parents and my origins, that I was playing a game by somebody else's rules" (p. 193). Why does Marji feel like the minute she progresses with one social group, she digresses with another? Is it possible to belong to two cultures simultaneously? Why or why not? If you have ELLs, recent immigrants, or biracial/bicultural students in your class, this is a great opportunity for them to share their personal experiences of belonging to two cultures.

Chapter: The Horse (pp. 198–206)

> In this chapter, we observe how Marji's relationship with her mother has evolved. As you mature, has your relationship with your parents changed? How?

Chapter: Hide & Seek (pp. 207–222)

In-Class Discussion: *Marji's Drug Career*

> Why does Marji initially get involved with drugs? Chart her drug usage up to this point. How does she become steadily more involved with drugs? What happens when Marji's teacher tries to help her? Why isn't he successful? How does Marji go from a casual user to a full-blown dealer? Is it a gradual or rapid process? What does she mean when she says "little by little, I became the portrait of Dorian Gray. The more time passed, the more I was marked" (p. 219). Who is Dorian Gray and how has she become like him?

In-Class Discussion: *Emigration Issues*

> How does Markus' mother react to their relationship? Compare her response to Mrs. Arrouas, her teacher's mother. What do their reactions illuminate about themselves?

Chapter: The Croissant (pp. 223–232)

In-Class Discussion: *Developing a Political Conscience*

> In this chapter, Marji emerges as a political activist. What are Marji's political beliefs? How do they differ from those held by Markus? Although most of you are not of voting age yet, you can still have political beliefs and participate in other political activities. Who are your local, state, and federal politicians? Choose one level of politics and research the incumbent's political platform, which reflects his/her beliefs. Do you agree or disagree with your elected politician's beliefs? Why or why not? How do his/her political beliefs affect/impact you or your family's everyday life? The class could engage in a debate with different students representing different voices of our elected officials (or if there's an upcoming election, students can represent the opponents' political beliefs).

Chapter: The Veil (pp. 233–245)

In-Class Discussion: *Becoming Someone*

> What does Marji mean when she says: "I think that I preferred to put myself in serious danger rather than confront my shame. My shame at not having become someone, the shame of not having

made my parents proud after all the sacrifices they had made for me. The shame of having become a mediocre nihilist" (p. 244)? Why is Marji ashamed? Do you think Marji is being hard on herself? Why or why not? Are you proud of the person you are? Why or why not?

Part 3: Back Home (pp. 246–341)

Chapter: The Return (pp. 246–257)

In-Class Discussion: *Coming Home as an Outsider*

Even though she is Iranian, do you think Marji adjusts easily to Iranian life? Why or why not? What happens when Marji revisits the room of her childhood? How has her perspective on life shifted? Look at the images on pages 250 and 251. How do the posters and graffiti of Tehran appear to Marji?

Chapter: The Joke (pp. 258–266)

In-Class Discussion: *Attitude Adjustment*

Analyze the phrase: "We can only feel sorry for ourselves when our misfortunes are still supportable . . . once this limit is crossed, the only way to bear the unbearable is to laugh at it" (p. 266). How does this realization help Marji deal with her problems? Do you agree or disagree? Have you ever felt this way in your own life? Share your stories with a partner or express it in your journal.

Chapter: Skiing (pp. 267–275)

In-Class Discussion: *Identity Crisis*

On page 272, Marji tells us, "I was a Westerner in Iran, an Iranian in the West. I had no identity. I didn't even know anymore why I was living." Why do you think Marji feels this way? Do you think she can resolve this conflict? How? If you were Marji's friend, what advice would you give her?

Chapter: The Exam (pp. 276–284)

In a Venn diagram, compare and contrast the difficulties of getting into college in Iran and in the USA. Do you share Marji's anxieties? Why or why not?

Chapter: The Makeup (pp. 285–291)

In this chapter, we learn how makeup transforms Marji's personality. Why do you think this is? Does makeup or getting dressed up have this effect on you? Why or why not?

Chapter: The Convocation (pp. 292–298)

In-Class Discussion: *The Crippling Power of Fear*

What does grandmother mean when she tells Marji that "it's fear that makes us lose our conscience. It's also what transforms us into cowards" (p. 298)? Why does fear make us lose our moral compass? How can it transform us into cowards? How has fear (or fearlessness) affected your own life?

Chapter: The Socks (pp. 299–311)

In-Class Discussion: *See the Detail, Lose the Picture*

On page 302, Marji tells us that the "regime had understood that one person leaving her house while asking herself: 'Are my trousers long enough?' 'Is my veil in place?' 'Can my makeup be seen?' 'Are they going to whip me?' no longer asks herself: 'Where is my freedom of thought?' 'Where is my freedom of speech?' 'What's going on in the political prisons?' 'My life, is it livable?'" (p. 302). How has the government used fear to distract the people? Are they successful? How do you avoid losing sight of the bigger picture in your own life?

Chapter: The Wedding (pp. 312–319)

In-Chapter Discussion: *Till Death Do Us Part*

Weddings are usually happy times for families. Analyze each family's members reaction to Marji's wedding. Pay close attention to the last panel on page 318. What do you think went wrong in Reza and Marji's marriage?

Chapter: The Satellite (pp. 320–327)

In-Chapter Discussion: *Political Conscience*

In this chapter, we learn about the First Gulf War. Discuss what Mr. Satrapi means when he says, "Personally, I hate Saddam and I have no sympathy for the Kuwaitis, but I hate just as much the cynicism of the allies who call themselves 'liberators' while they're there for the oil" (p. 322). He compares this incident with Afghanistan, which "no one lifted a finger because [it's] poor . . . " With this statement, Mr. Satrapi argues that the First Gulf War is

> **One Step Further**
>
> To encourage political conscientiousness in your students, consider the U.S. wars in Afghanistan and Iraq. Mimicking the 9/11 Commission, create a War on Terrorism Commission. Assign your students roles such as: Congress, the military, the American public, and the president. Have your students research both wars and debate its pros and cons and present their findings to the Commission.

not about human rights, but oil. Do you agree or disagree? Why does Marji believe that it is important to have a political conscience and not be lost "in a cloud of happiness"? Explore your own political conscience.

Chapter: The End (pp. 328–341)

In-Class Discussion: *Women's Rights*

Why does Marji suddenly decide that she must leave Iran? What rights do Iranian women have and not have? How deeply are women's rights abused? How does Behzad, the illustrator, treat his wife? How does this reflect the larger social-political issues?

In-Class Discussion: *The Price of Freedom*

As she leaves her family in the airport, Marji tells us that "freedom had a price." What price does Marji pay? Does all freedom have a price? Have you paid a price for freedom?

Post-Reading Activity: Another Brick in the Wall

Peter Sis' Caldecott-winning book *The Wall: Growing Up Behind the Iron Curtain* is an autobiographical account of his life growing up in Czechoslovakia during the Cold War. Because of its short length, this picture book is the perfect work to compare and contrast with *Persepolis*. For your convenience, a printable guide for this activity ("Persepolis & The Wall") has been provided in the Appendix.

As you read *The Wall*, point out to your students that the two stories are being told simultaneously: the caption text documents events occurring outside of the author's life, while the centered text tells Sis' own personal story. Then, using the guides, have your students compare and contrast Marjane Satrapi's and Peter Sis' stories:

• What are the political associations and beliefs of the authors' parents?

- How do both regimes acquire and retain power?

- How are the children of the regimes indoctrinated?

- How does each of the governments deal with insurgency?

- How do the authors view Western culture?

- What role do the arts play in both authors' lives?

- How do the authors resist the authorities?

- How does Marji's story reflect her experience as a young woman? How does Peter's story reflect his experience as a young man?

- What is the current government in both countries?

- Why do you think Czechoslovakia (now the Czech Republic and Slovakia respectively) eventually becomes a democracy while Iran does not?

One Step Further

The arts greatly inspired Peter Sis' political activism. Explore this connection further by considering the Cold War from the American perspective. Fearful of their Soviet counterparts, American policymakers encouraged a strong anti-Soviet sentiment. A few artists (Pete Seeger, Bob Dylan, Nena, Sting, for example) encouraged an end to the Soviet hysteria in their music. Listen to some of their music in class. Discuss its consequences: How has music served as a form of social protest? Does such music exist today?

CHAPTER SEVEN

Power Wars

A Maus at Fahrenheit 451

Let you alone! That's all very well, but how can I leave myself alone? We need not to be let alone. We need to be really bothered once in a while. How long is it been since you were *really* bothered? About something important, about something real? — Guy Montag in *Fahrenheit 451* (Bradbury, 1953/1987, p. 52)

Washing one's hands of the conflict between the powerful and the powerless means to side with the powerful, not to be neutral. (Freire, 1985, p. 122)

Why Talk about Power?

Power is a part of all of our lives. Whether we are conscious of it or not, the political system we are part of, the friends we socialize with, the schools we attend, all generate and perpetuate specific and nuanced power dynamics. Sometimes power is achieved in democratic ways, other times it is seized violently without consent. By becoming aware of the nature of power and the social structures it creates, we can learn how to navigate and challenge the various power systems we are a part of.

This unit focuses specifically on the relationships between governments and their people. Generally, people monitor governments while governments monitor people. While this relationship is dynamic and fluid, it is also at the foundational core of any functioning society. Whether it is protesting the Freedom of Information Act, Tea Partiers rallying against big government policies, or Occupy Wall Street fighting the "1 percent," Americans are constantly monitoring their individual rights. This is not the case in many other countries. In China, political activists are closely supervised and oftentimes imprisoned. In Burma, civilians are forced to carry wounded soldiers through areas containing landmines. In Burundi, homosexuality is outlawed and considered a criminal offense. While international human rights organizations continue to protest these violations of individual rights, this has not always been the case. There have been moments in modern history when the world was silent to the abuses of others.

One recent example of this is the Holocaust. Between 1938 and 1945, 11 million people, of whom one million were children, were systematically terrorized and murdered. Though the Holocaust permanently changed the face of world Jewry, it cannot be categorized solely as a Jewish historical event; instead it should be viewed as a period of inexplicable silence, a brutal silence that powerfully impacted the history of the entire world. In order to understand how civilized governments encouraged the mass murder of millions, we must analyze the power structures, social issues, and cultural prejudices that lead the perpetrators of the Holocaust to consciously ignore the basic rights of millions of human beings.

Proponents of critical literacy refuse to bury the ashes of the past. We believe that the world cannot be allowed to forget, to ever again be silent to the suffering of others. In this interconnected world, we are all safeguards of human rights. Critical literacy believes that history plays a real role in our civil consciousness and reminds us that blind prejudice, absolute power, and social indifference can never be tolerated.

How Do I Use This Unit?

In this unit, we explore how government power impacts individual lives. While both these works center on personal narratives, they are totally different. The first text, Ray Bradbury's *Fahrenheit 451* (1953/1987), is set in a futuristic fictional America; while the second text, Art Spiegelman's *The Complete Maus* (1997), documents the Holocaust experience of the author's father. In both *Fahrenheit 451* and *Maus*, the lead characters are persecuted by seemingly omnipotent authorities. In their refusal to submit, in their stories of survival, each hero challenges and ultimately reclaims power.

By presenting two extreme cases, both of these stories contain important messages about the nature and workings of power. In the fictional world of *Fahrenheit 451*, eerily reminiscent of our own, books are forbidden. The novel explores how a fireman (in this case a book burner) accidentally reads a line from a book and as a result, is inspired to risk everything to fight state-sponsored censorship. In *Maus*, the extreme is taken to parody. Following the racist ideology of the time, each ethnic group is caricaturized as another animal. The graphic novel documents how the author's father, portrayed as a mouse, is nearly exterminated by the Nazis, portrayed as cats, simply because he is a Jew. *Fahrenheit 451*, a National Book Award winner, is essentially a book about books. It chronicles the important role books play in correcting imbalances of power. Though first printed in 1953, its themes and messages remain extremely relevant today. *Maus*, the first graphic novel to win a Pulitzer Prize, is also referential of itself as a medium. In fact, many comic enthusiasts consider *Maus* to be the first real graphic novel, having redefined the visual literary art form in new ways. We recommend that you take the time to acknowledge the media of both these texts. This will allow your students to reflect not only on their own literacy practices, but encourage new ones.

Text 1: *Fahrenheit 451* by Ray Bradbury

A classic high school text, *Fahrenheit 451* offers brilliant insights into humanity's need and love for the printed word.

What Is *Fahrenheit 451* About?

Fahrenheit 451 explores the delicate relationship between governments and people. Specifically, it documents how an unsupervised government turns its back on its people and ultimately encourages submission through state-sanctioned mindlessness. The main character, Guy Montag, is a fireman responsible for burning books along with the homes (and people) that house them. After meeting a young woman, Guy is stirred to consciousness and questions his society's mass conformity. He embarks on a quest for individuality and creative wakefulness, which ultimately leads him to rebel against his society.

Lesson Opener: Burning Books

Over the years, many books have been challenged and banned in the United States. A challenged book is when a group objects to the content of a book and attempts to have it removed from libraries or a school curriculum. A banned book is considered an offensive book that is actually removed and/or restricted. Ironically, *Fahrenheit 451* not only explores this issue of censorship, but has been subject to it as well. This activity aims to explore these ideas. For your convenience, a printable guide for this activity ("Burning Books") has been provided in the Appendix.

With your students, discuss the following questions:

- Define censorship and give an example.

- Why do you think someone would want to challenge/ban a book?

- Can a book really be dangerous? To whom? How?

- How could literacy pose a threat to those in power?

One Step Further

Some of the most frequently challenged books are: *The Bluest Eye* by Toni Morrison; *Of Mice and Men* by John Steinbeck; *A Light in the Attic* by Shel Silverstein; *I Know Why the Caged Bird Sings* by Maya Angelou; *The Adventures of Huckleberry Finn* by Mark Twain; the Harry Potter series by J. K. Rowling; *Fallen Angels* by Walter Dean Myers; *In the Night Kitchen* by Maurice Sendak; and *The Outsiders* by S.E. Hinton. If your class has read any of these books, divide the class into debate groups and have them prepare arguments for or against a particular book. Explain to students that they will be acting as a school board deciding whether or not to allow a book to be studied in an elementary/junior high/high school. If they have not read any of these books, do a read-aloud of one of the shorter books (like *Heather Has Two Mommies* or *In the Night Kitchen*). After the students debate the book, have them cast a vote and discuss the results.

When *Fahrenheit 451* was reprinted in 1967, the publishers created a special edition to be sold to high schools. Without informing Bradbury or putting a note in the edition, the publisher removed all "bad" words from the novel. The expurgated edition was sold for 13 years before Bradbury found out about it. Eventually, the publisher withdrew the version and replaced it with the original. The publicity generated by this incident caused the American Library Association's Intellectual Freedom Committee to investigate other school books and use its considerable economic clout to warn publishers that any excised versions of books must be clearly identified.

Explain that *censorship* is enacted when an authority or society deems certain materials to be harmful and authorizes their removal. Discuss if censorship is ever justified. Interestingly, in *Fahrenheit 451*, it is the people themselves who reject books because reading interferes with their happiness. So, while the government created this rule, it is the people who enabled and embraced it. Ask students to describe situations in which they felt censored. Critical literacy focuses on students rediscovering, creating, and recreating meanings of a word by personally relating to it. For example, in our lessons, students reported being censored by school policies or teachers based on the language or words they use, or the clothes they wear; or, at home where certain TV programs, video games, or films are prohibited; or, by friends where peer pressure prevents them from behaving, talking, or dressing as their authentic selves, or befriending others who are in the margins. Students can debate and argue for or against censorship citing concrete examples to support their position.

Together, discuss:

- Have you ever been affected by censorship? If so, share your experience.

- Why do you think a society would choose to ban books?

- Why would the government encourage a society to do so?

- Is the act of banning books a form of "policing" your thoughts?

- Do books still play this role or have other media assumed this purpose?

Teachers should reference current events that reflect the practice of banning books or other media. For example, in 2012, Tucson high schools in Arizona banned all works that reflected themes of oppression, race, and ethnicity, including Shakespeare's *The Tempest*.

Pre-Reading Activity: First Amendment Rights

In this activity, we explore the issue of censorship more deeply. We do this by reading the coda from the 1979 edition of *Fahrenheit 451*. This excerpt has been provided in the Appendix.

Begin this activity by examining the first amendment of the U.S. Constitution. Discuss freedom of speech, freedom of the press, and the right to protest. Have your students explore recent examples of First Amendment issues addressed in the courts. Then, discuss:

- How did different groups respond to what was said/done?

- Why do you think they responded in such a way?

- Do you agree or disagree with the reactions to what was said/done?

- What do you think would have been a better reaction to what was said/done?

- How do you define the First Amendment in your own life?

- How do you define it in regard to others?

- Should there be parameters to the First Amendment? If so, who should create and enforce those parameters?

- What do you think Bradbury would say about First Amendment rights and this issue?

Afterwards, read the Coda from *Fahrenheit 451* and discuss the following questions:

- What do you think Bradbury means when he says "there is more than one way to burn a book"?

- How does Bradbury define "minorities"?

- Why would minorities want to challenge/ban/edit books?

- Bradbury's play is a creative reinvention of a classic. Why did the university refuse to put it on? Do you agree or disagree with the university's decision? Why?

- How does Bradbury feel about their reasoning?

- Do you agree or disagree with Bradbury?

- What does Bradbury tell minorities who disagree with his work to do?

- What are the "beheadings, finger-choppings, [and] lung-deflations" symbolic of? How is Bradbury saying he feels about imposed editing?

- What does Bradbury mean when he says "I will not go gently onto the shelf, degutted, to become a non-book"? Degutted by whom? What does it mean to be a "non-book"?

- How does Bradbury seem to define a book? Do you agree or disagree? Explain.

- What "game" is Bradbury referring to in the last paragraph? Who are the "umpires" and "referees"? By using this analogy, what is he telling us about books?

READING ACTIVITIES: Questions & Discussion Topics

It is very important for lessons to be rooted in the text. According to research, many students lack good textual analytical skills. To address this deficit, critical literacy, which tends to explore generative themes, must also be grounded in real textual examples. To balance these two goals, we have created both reading comprehension questions and in-class discussion topics/activities that include critical textual analysis. To encourage your own growth as an educator, comprehension questions have only been provided for the first part of the book. We have also provided discussion topics for the entire text. To save class time, we recommend the questions be done for homework, and class time be used for the in-class discussions and activities.

Part I: The Hearth and the Salamander (pp. 3–68)

1. Reflect on the title. What is a hearth? How does a salamander react to fire? What do you think this chapter will be about?

2. How does *Fahrenheit 451* begin?

3. Who is Guy Montag? What does he do for a living?

4. Why is the number "451" imprinted on Guy's helmet? What does it mean?

5. How does Guy feel about his job?

6. Who does Guy see on his way home from work?

7. Who is Clarisse? Is she afraid of Guy? Why or why not?

8. Analyze the phrase (p. 7) "He saw himself in her eyes, suspended in two . . . "

9. What does Guy experience while talking to Clarisse?

10. How does Guy describe his job to Clarisse? Does he feel differently about his job now?

11. Why do you think books are outlawed?

12. How has the job of a fireman changed from the way we know it?

13. On page. 9, Clarisse tells Montag: "I sometimes think drivers don't know what grass is, or flowers, because they never see them slowly . . . . If you showed a driver a green blur, Oh yes! He'd say, that's grass! A pink blur! That's a rose garden! White blurs are houses. Brown blurs are cows." What does this tell you about the society? Are there any parallels with our own? How so?

14. On page 9, Montag tells Clarisse: "You think too many things." Does she? Does Clarisse seem different from the others? How? What evidence is there that she is different?

15. What facts does Clarisse share with Montag? Does he know these things? How does he react?

In-Class Discussion: *Non-Mainstream Values*

What is Clarisse's family like? Do they value the same things as the society? How does their society treat Clarisse and her family? Discuss: Does our society have mainstream values? If so, what are they? How do we deal with people with different values? To facilitate this discussion, use recent media articles (for example the 2008 debate over the 400 children belonging to a polygamist group in Texas).

1. On page 10, Guy compares Clarisse to a clock and a mirror. Why?

2. Describe Guy's home life. How does Guy feel in his home? Why?

3. What is Guy's wife, Mildred, like? Compare her to Clarisse.

4. What has Mildred done? Why do you think she did it?

5. Describe the machine used to save Mildred's life.

In-Class Discussion: *Welcome to the Machine*

On page 14, Guy tells us that the machine used to save Mildred's life "had an Eye. The impersonal operator of the machine could, by wearing a special optical helmet, gaze into the soul of the person whom he was pumping out." What is this passage telling us? Can the machine actually see the soul of a person? Do you think Mildred has a soul? How is she like a machine?

Describe the men operating the machine. Why did the hospital not send doctors? What does this tell us about the society? On page 16, "Nobody knows anyone. Strangers come and violate you. Strangers come and cut your heart out. Strangers come and take your blood. Good God, who *were* these men? I never saw them before in my *life*." What is the technology in this society like? Are there any parallels to our own society?

1. Why does Mildred refuse to accept that she had tried to kill herself?

2. Describe the TV screens in Montag's house. How does Mildred feel about them? How does Guy feel about them?

3. What does Clarisse's "dandelion test" prove? Is Guy in love with Mildred? Why does Guy struggle to accept the truth?

4. Why does Clarisse seem older than Mildred? What does she have that Mildred does not?

5. In French, *clarisse* means bright. What brightness does Clarisse bring to Guy's life?

In-Class Discussion: *Self-Reflection & Inner Conflict*

What is reflection? What is self-reflection? Why is the ability to self-reflect so important? Why do you think this society decided to refrain from reflecting on itself (remember no one is allowed to ask "why," only "how")? For the first time in a long time, Montag is reflecting on himself. His reflection results in inner conflict. For the first time, Guy realizes that he has been living a shallow (if not false) life. He realizes that he is not happy. Suddenly, Guy's whole world is plunged into chaos. Is his whole life a lie? On page 24, he describes this feeling: "He felt his body divide itself into a hotness and a coldness, a softness and a hardness, a trembling and a not trembling, the two halves grinding one upon the other." What are the two halves? Why are they pulling him in different directions? How does Guy deal with his inner conflict?

> ## One Step Further
> In a journal entry, reflect on your own experiences with inner conflict. How did it resolve?

1. How does Guy feel about the Mechanical Hound?

2. What does he compare the Hound to? Why?

3. Is the Mechanical Hound dead or alive?

4. What is the Mechanical Hound's function? What was it made to do?

In-Class Discussion: *Society & and Violence*

Societies create both schools and technology. How does Clarisse describe school? What does school have in common with the Mechanical Hound? On page 30, Clarisse says "I'm afraid of children my own age. They kill each other. Did it always use to be this way? My uncle says no. Six of my friends have been shot in the last year alone. Ten of them died in car wrecks. I'm afraid of them and they don't like me because I'm afraid." This society is decidedly violent. Kids kill kids, robot dogs sniff out free thinkers and inject them with sedatives, and firemen burn people along with their books. Why do you think this society has become so violent? What about our own society? To facilitate a discussion, discuss school violence, using Columbine as an example. Why is our own society becoming increasingly violent?

1. What happens to Clarisse?

2. When Clarisse is not there to walk Guy home, his routine is broken. Why is this significant?

3. With his habit broken, what does Guy begin to do?

4. What does Captain Beatty say is the history of firemen?

5. Was Benjamin Franklin really a fireman? What is the author trying to tell us? How can governments use books as control mechanisms? Why would they want to?

In-Class Discussion: *The Life of Objects*

During the fire, Captain Beatty claims that books are just objects; they don't feel or get hurt. Do you agree or disagree? Can an object, like a book, "feel"? Can it have a life? Compare to Mildred's TVs. Why does she call the actors "relatives"? Does the TV have life to Mildred?

1. By running into the fire, the woman breaks the firemen's fire pattern. How does this encourage Guy's questioning?

2. How would you describe Captain Beatty? Are you surprised that he quoted from a book?

3. On page 41, what "poison" is Guy referring to?

4. Is it significant that Mildred and Guy can't remember where they met? Why?

5. What does Mildred say happened to Clarisse? Do you think she cares? Why or why not? Compare her reaction to Guy's? Are they different? How?

6. How does Mildred react to Guy's sickness? Why?

In-Class Discussion: *Guy's Transformation Begins*

When Guy comes home from burning the woman and her books, something has changed for him. He notices Mildred and sees her differently. What has changed? How is he different? Mildred does not react (she can't feel) when Guy tells her that he helped burn a woman with her books. He tells her: "last night I thought about all the kerosene I've used in the past ten years. And I thought about books. And for the first time I realized that a man was behind each one of those books. A man had to think them up. A man had to take a long time to put them down on paper. And I never even thought that thought before . . . . It took some man a lifetime maybe to put some of his thoughts down, looking around at the world and life, and then I came along in two minutes and boom! It's all over" (p. 52). What has Guy realized (return to discussion about life of objects)? Is he feeling guilty for the one woman he burned?

For the first time in a long time, Guy is truly bothered by something; he feels bad about something he did. On page 52, he asks Mildred "How long is it since you were *really* bothered? About something important, about something real?" Do you think you are more like Mildred or Guy? Why is it so hard to empathize with injustices? Do other people's sufferings bother you? Why or why not? When was the last time you were bothered, *really* bothered by something real?

1. Who comes to visit Guy?

2. Is Captain Beatty surprised by Guy's "sickness"? What do you think Guy is really sick from?

In-Class Discussion: *The Roots of Censorship*

How does Captain Beatty explain the history of books to Guy? Why did people used to read? What were their reading experiences like? Why did reading change? Who began suppressing books (refer to discussion of "minorities" in pre-reading activity) and why? According to Captain Beatty, why did people stop reading? How did the education system change? Books promote free thinking, which encourages people to think on their own and create their own paths in life. This society chose conformity over individuality. Why? Why do you think the government encouraged the people to ban books? And for what purpose? Who benefits? Who does it hurt?

1. Refer back to Bradbury's definition of minorities. Why do certain groups want to ban certain books?

2. How does Captain Beatty explain Clarisse's "differences"? How did they happen?

3. How does Captain Beatty keep defining "peace"? What is his "peace"? Do you think that it's really peaceful?

4. What does Captain Beatty think of books?

5. How does Guy react to Captain Beatty's visit?

6. What has Guy hidden in his air conditioner shaft? Why do you think he's done this?

7. How does Mildred react? Why?

8. What does Guy decide to do with the books? Does Mildred agree or disagree with his plan?

Part 2: The Sieve and the Sand (pp. 71–110)

In-Class Discussion: *Information and Society*

On page 87, Faber tells Guy that three things are missing from society: (1) quality information, (2) the leisure to digest it, and (3) the right to carry out actions based on what we learn from the interaction of the first two. What does this mean? What has society lost? Are these three elements present in our own society? Do we have access to quality information? Do we have time to process that information? And do we exercise the right to act based on that quality information? To facilitate discussion, take a current issue in the media (war in Iraq, political elections) and identity these three elements. What happens when one of these elements is missing (like when we don't receive quality information)?

In-Class Discussion: *"Dover Beach"*

Guy reads the last two stanzas of Mathew Arnold's "Dover Beach." Read the entire poem. What is this poem about? What is "pathetic fallacy" and how does Arnold use it? How does the definition of the sea change? Why do you think Bradbury had Guy read *this* particular poem at *this* particular part of his journey?

In-Class Discussion: *The Test*

Guy, the hero in *Fahrenheit 451*, is now faced with the ultimate test. Describe Guy's mental state. Does he want to continue burning things? What does Captain Beatty want him to do? Why? Do you think Guy will do it? Have you ever been faced with a "test" that totally challenged your values? How did you react?

Part 3: Burning Bright (pp. 113–165)

In-Class Discussion: *Becoming an Authentic Person*

At his home, Guy fully turns his back on his society's values by murdering Captain Beatty, two firemen, and the Mechanical Hound. He also "kills" Faber by burning the earpiece (the "voice") that Faber gave him. For the first time, Guy is completely on his own. He is no longer influenced by those around him. What does this tell us about becoming an independent person? Is it easy to "break free" from the voices of influence? Are you an authentic person? Do you make your own thought-out decisions or do you mindlessly follow or listen to others?

In-Class Discussion: *Finding a Life Path*

Now that he has become his own authentic person, Guy can begin to lead an honest and true life. Why do you think Guy suddenly craves farm life? What is represented by "farm life"? What path does Guy find? What "path" is this symbolic of? Why does Guy believe Clarisse has walked on the same path? What is a life path? Do they have destinations? Do you have a life path? Do you have a destination? What choices and circumstances led you to discovering who you were and your own life journey?

In-Class Discussion: *Internalization*

There are no papers or physical books in the rebels' camps. The men are the books. The books live inside the men. What does this tell us about the nature of reading? How should books be read? Compare this to your own reading process. How do you read? Do you internalize your readings? Why is real reading "internalized" reading?.

In-Class Discussion: *Encouraging a Society That Self-Reflects*

Granger tells Guy that he and the other rebels are "remembering" for society (p. 164). What do you think this means? What are they remembering? For whom? Why is it so important to remember? Granger tells Guy that the first thing they will build after the war will be a mirror factory and for a whole year they will do nothing but "put out mirrors" (p. 164). Why mirrors? Refer back to when Guy compared Clarisse to a mirror. What do mirrors represent? Why does this society need mirrors so badly? Why is reflection so important? Does our society reflect on its actions? Does the government? To facilitate a discussion, use current issues (such as the war in Iraq, the Occupy Wall Street protests) and discuss if our government and society has adequately reflected on its position/purpose/objectives.

Post-Reading Activity: Are We TV Addicts?

Bradbury has stated that *Fahrenheit 451* is a story about how television destroys interest in reading literature, which ultimately leads to ignorance of total facts. In *Fahrenheit 451*, the society has abandoned books in favor of hollow entertainment and instant gratification. Every home has a TV that fills the walls and dominates their lives. In *Fahrenheit 451*, this is taken to an extreme, and TV (and its characters) has replaced the need for real family. For your convenience, a printable copy of the survey has been included in the Appendix.

Begin the activity by having your students take the survey on their TV habits. After completing it, share the results with the class. Discuss that according to Nielsen research, the average American teen watches about three and a half hours of TV every day or about 24 hours a week (Nielsen, 2010). Such an individual, assuming they maintain this practice after adolescence, will spend roughly 81,000 hours watching TV or about a decade of their entire life. Reflect on these findings:

• Do you think these findings (both class and national) are problematic? Why?

• Should we be watching this much TV? Why or why not?

• Compare our society's TV habits with Bradbury's.

- What does the author warn us about excess TV watching? What can it affect?

- Do you agree or disagree with Bradbury's view? Why or why not?

- Do you think we are addicted to entertainment? Explain.

Action is always the bottom line. It is not enough to simply feel a certain way; we must act or risk living a life of hypocrisy. For those of your students who share the sentiment, discuss ways of limiting television watching. Explore other activities that are both *educational* and *entertaining*. For those kids who are really committed, ask them to engage in an experiment: to turn off their TV for a week. If possible, have them record their week (either by creating webcasts or journaling). When were their temptations highest? How did they feel as the week progressed? What other things did they do? At the end of the week, have them share their experiences with the class.

One Step Further

In addition to watching programs, Americans watch thousands of commercials a year. The average American child views 20,000 TV commercials a year (that's without billboards and ads) (Herr, 2007). Research has also shown that children can develop brand loyalty by the age of two. In *Fahrenheit 451*, the society is constantly bombarded by advertisements, on the train and gigantic billboards. In a research assignment, ask your students to document the types of commercials they see on TV. They should keep track of the products portrayed, the frequency of the commercial, its success (was it an influencing commercial?) and the audience. In school, compare the results and discuss emergent patterns.

1. How are commercials produced to be both entertaining and convincing?

2. Do commercials influence your purchases? How?

3. Do you think commercials really depict reality?

4. What are advertisers hoping you'll not only buy but "buy into"?

5. Examine the causes of excess TV watching. Why does the society in *Fahrenheit 451* watch so much TV? What are their reasons? Why do you think we as a society are watching so much TV?

Teachers can include social media (Facebook, Twitter, iPhone/Androids, iPad and so forth in their analysis.

Text 2: *Maus I & II* by Art Spiegelman

Like many graphic novels, *Maus* defies genre; it is a memoir, an autobiography, bildungsroman, and comic. With pictures and words, *Maus* provides a multidimensional experience, making it a compelling medium through which one can analyze the Holocaust and its global and individual consequences. Unlike first-person narratives, the author in retelling his father's story must address his own story and construct his identity from the ashes of the past. A quick note about reading graphic novels: do not assume that your students will be able to read this text proficiently. Many will initially read either the words or pictures, which will prevent them from grasping the full narrative weight of the text. To avoid this, prepare reading activities that scaffold them throughout this process and guide them in reading both modes simultaneously. We recommend giving students time in class to read independently and then having them work in groups to discuss what they have read. We have found that this structure supports students in their meaning-making process while allowing them to read at their own pace.

> ### What Is *Maus* About?
> Told in brilliant graphic form, *Maus* documents the author's father's incredible story of survival of WWII. In transcribing his father's journey, the author is forced to face his own demons and find purpose in his life.

Lesson Opener: Caricaturizing History

One of the most noticeable characteristics of *Maus I & II* is its use of animals to depict people. This parodies much of the Nazi propaganda of the early twentieth century.

Introduce this topic by showing your students historical samples of Nazi propaganda. Ask them why they think these caricatures successfully enforced Nazi ideology. Explain that *Maus* uses caricature in a similarly powerful way. In groups, have your students preview the text, identifying key animal types and characters. Then, have them discuss how these caricatures play a role in solidifying stereotypes.

To create a personal connection to this idea, ask your students to draw a caricature of themselves as an animal and write a brief explanation of their drawing. Explain that in *Understanding Comics*, comic writer Scott McCloud (1993) argues that "a face drawn with great detail can represent only one specific person, but that a face drawn with few details—a smiley face, for instance—could be almost anyone" (p. 31). Either together or in groups, have your students describe the faces in *Maus* to decide if they are iconic (could be anyone) or particular (could only be the one person). Brainstorm why the author chose to portray his characters in this way.

If many students are familiar with comics, anime, or graphic novels, ask those students to share their expertise with the class. Encourage students to include any knowledge they have about comic books and whether or not Spiegelman satisfies or challenges conventions. Skimming through the text, give specific instructions to notice the frames (the lines around the panels) and the gutters (space between the frames). There are many "bleeds" in the text, making Spiegelman's drawing style seem "unprofessional." He also drew *Maus* to scale (as opposed to twice the size and then shrinking it), which affected the overall clarity of the work. Together, discuss why the author would choose to draw his work in this way.

Pre-Reading Activity: Survey the Text

This activity expands on the ideas raised in the lesson opener. It elaborates on the author's drawing style, tying it directly to his parents' Holocaust experience. For your convenience, a printable guide for this activity ("Understanding *Maus*") has been provided in the Appendix.

Either in groups or together, have your students read what Art Spiegelman (1994) has said about *Maus*:

> *Maus*, my comic book about my parents' life in Hitler's Europe, which uses cats to represent Germans and mice to represent Jews, was made in collaboration with Hitler. (Now will I have to share my Pulitzer?) It was the Nazis' idea to divvy the human race up into species, into *Übermenschen* and *Untermenschen*, to "exterminate" (as opposed to murder) Jews like vermin, to use Zyklon B—a pesticide—in the gas chambers. My anthropomorphized mice carry trace elements of Fips's anti-Semitic Jew-as-rat cartoons for *Der Stürmer*, but by being particularized they are invested with personhood; they stand upright and affirm their humanity. Cartoons personalize; they give specific form to stereotypes.

To help guide your students' discussions, have them respond to the following questions:

- What does the author mean when he says *Maus* was written in "collaboration with Hitler"?

- Who are the *übermenschen* and *untermenschen*?

- Are people comparable to rodents and bugs? Why?

- The author decides to make the mice personable and give them a sense of humanity. How do you think he does this? Is he successful? Why or why not?

- Does the use of animals create sympathy or feelings of indifference? Do these depictions trivialize the events of the time period?

Reading Activity: Questions & Discussion Topics

It is very important for lessons to be rooted in the text. According to research, many students lack good textual analytical skills. To address this deficit, critical literacy, which tends to explore generative themes, must also be grounded in real textual examples. To balance these two goals, we have created both reading comprehension questions and in-class discussion topics/activities that include critical textual analysis. To encourage your own growth as an educator, comprehension questions have been provided only for the first part of the book. We have also provided discussion topics for the entire text. To save class time, we recommend the questions be done for homework, and class time be used for the in-class discussions and activities.

Maus I: The Sheik

1. Where does *Maus* take place?

2. About how many years after the Holocaust is the author writing *Maus*?

3. What is the author's relationship with his father?

4. Who is Mala? Describe her relationship with Vladek.

5. Why do you think the author's father is constantly riding an exercise bike? What do you think it is symbolic of?

6. Who is "the sheik"? Why is it the title of the chapter?

In-Class Discussion: *The Rain in Spain . . .*

What did you notice about the language or dialects of the text? Do any of the characters have accents? How does this change your image of Vladek? In general, how do our accents make us unique? Are accents a signifier of one's ability or intelligence level? Share stories. If you have ELLs or students with accents in your class, ask them to share any personal stories of language or dialect bias against them. According to research, linguistic and dialectical "-isms" have been largely uncontested and overlooked areas where bias, judgment, and discrimination occur. Sharing stories of how students from this diverse population have been treated based on how they speak and sound will shed awareness and sensitivity to others not experiencing this type of "-ism."

> **One Step Further**
> Analyze the language and dialectical diversity within the classroom. Encourage students to speak of their accents and how they obtained them. Accents are part of who we are and where we come from. They are part of our "identity package." Discuss this issue and its social ramifications. Do some accents appear "smarter" or "dumber" and if so, why? And by whom?

Maus I: The Honeymoon

1. Why do you think Vladek takes so many pills?

2. What was Anja (the author's mother) secretly?

3. Why are people so scared to be involved with "the Communists"?

4. How are the Polish police depicted? Why?

5. Why do you think Spiegelman uses cats to represent the Nazis? What stereotype is he playing into?

6. What happened to the author's mother?

7. The sanitarium is described as a place "far away from everything . . . so peaceful . . . so quiet" how does this contrast with what the Spiegelmans return home to?

Maus I: Prisoner of War

1. Why do you think Vladek makes his son, the author, finish his plate?

2. Describe Vladek's thoughts when he is commanded to shoot the Nazis. How do his feelings change after he is captured? Are there times when killing is justified? Explain.

3. Why does the S.S. soldier make a big deal when he finds so much cash on Vladek? What stereotype is playing into it?

4. Why were the Jewish prisoners treated less fairly than the Polish prisoners? Is there a social hierarchy present? If so, what is it?

> **One Step Further**
> Think about your own identity. Is it something constant or changing? Do we "don different masks" at different times and if so, why? Why would someone choose to be someone they're not? (An example of this would be "Black Skin, White Masks." Are there times when people "act White" or "act Black" or "act rich" or "act poor"?) Are certain social groups more powerful at different times (think: Congress and the basketball court)? How can we stay true to ourselves at all times?

In-Class Discussion

On page 64, the Jewish characters wear masks. From this point on, various characters at different times, will disguise as other animals. What do you think the author is trying to say about identity? Look on the back flap of the book; what is the author wearing? Why?

Maus I: The Noose Tightens

1. On page 77, what is Vladek wearing for the first time in the book? Why do you think the Nazis insisted that it be worn at all times?

2. What difficult situation is the family faced with?

3. Describe life in the ghetto. Are the conditions humane?

4. What happened to Anja's grandparents?

5. At the stadium, what basic human rights were violated?

Maus I: Mouse Holes

1. Notice the title of this chapter. What do you think it foreshadows?

In-Class Discussion

The "comic in the comic" is a kind of flashback. Notice the different drawing style. What effect does it have? Why do you think the author is wearing prison stripes and blames his dead mother for "committing the perfect crime"? What kind of insight does it give you? Why do you think the author has included it? How do you think it will change the rest of the story?

1. What was it like for children living in the ghetto?

2. Did Vladek's family know about Auschwitz? Did they believe the rumors? Why?

3. High-stress situations either bring out the best in people or the worst in people. Describe a character who rose to the occasion and another who fell short.

4. War is expensive. Why couldn't Anja's father's millions of dollars save him?

5. What happens to Vladek's son, Richieu?

Maus I: Mouse Trap

1. Notice the title of this chapter. What do you think it's about?

2. On page 133, the author and his father have a conversation about comic books. Why does the author think that "Maus" will be a different type of comic book that "even people who don't usually read such stories will be interested"?

3. What happens when Anja and Vladek try to go back to their old house?

4. Is Motonowa a righteous gentile? Why or why not?

5. On page 147, the Spiegelmans encounter a mouse. How does Anja react? Why do you think this is so significant?

6. Why do you think the Jews speak Yiddish in front of the smugglers?

7. Describe the Spiegelmans' arrival at Auschwitz. What do they realize?

8. Think back on the "comic in a comic"; why do you think Vladek destroyed Anja's diaries?

9. Is Art right to get so upset? Is his father really a "murderer"? Compare to the "comic in a comic" when Art accuses his mother of being a murderer, too.

In-Class Discussion

Look at page 159, at the fourth panel. What does the jagged speech balloon mean? Why do you think that? Look at the next panel. What is the meaning of the black squiggle over Art's head? Look at the very last panel. Why is there no frame? What details do you notice about that panel? Artie's back is turned, he's carrying a satchel, and he seems to be smoking. What feelings does this frame express?

In-Class Discussion

On page 159, when Art leaves, his father calls out to him "Don't be such a stranger!" Is Art's father a stranger to him? Why? Even though none of us has the same background or life experiences, we do not need to be strangers. How can we avoid feeling like strangers? What does it mean to be part of a community and how can we create that atmosphere in our classroom?

Maus II: Mauschwitz & Auschwitz (time flies)

In-Class Discussion: *Text Structure*

Look at page 41; what do the words tell us has happened? What do the pictures tell us? How many different things are the pictures trying to tell? How has the chronology of the story changed? What has happened to Vladek? On page 42, the author shrinks and grows again. Why?

In-Class Discussion

On page 43, the author writes that Dr. Pavel's "place is overrun with stray dogs and cats" and wonders, "Can I mention this, or does it completely screw up my metaphor?" What is the metaphor? Does it "screw up" the author's metaphor?

In-Class Discussion: *I Know What You're Going Through . . .*

Our experiences shape our lives. Think of your own experiences; how have they changed your life? Art tries to understand his father's history by visiting Dr. Pavel. Is he able to? Is it possible for us to understand each other's experiences?

Maus II: . . . And Here My Troubles Began

In-Class Discussion: *The Golden Rule*

Even though Vladek has experienced discrimination firsthand, it does not stop him from acting discriminatorily. Today, no one makes people wear yellow stars, and yet we still discriminate against one another. What does discrimination look like today? Give examples. Is discrimination obvious, subtle, or both? Explain. Have you, or someone you know, ever been discriminated against? Describe your feelings. Do you, or anyone you know, harbor any anger or hatred towards the person, or members of that particular group, who discriminated against you?

Maus II: Saved

In-Class Discussion: *Bleeding Hearts*

Notice the bleed on page 115. What effect does the never-ending stack of family photographs have? What is the author telling us about the people in his family (and their histories) who have been lost?

Maus II: The Second Honeymoon

In-Class Discussion: *A Photo Is More Powerful than Words*

In book two there are actual photos. How are these images different from the drawings? How do you feel when you see photographs of Richieu and Vladek? (Refer to the previous questions drawn from Scott McCloud's argument.) Try to explain the author's reasons. Consider the popular idiom, "a picture is worth a thousand words." *Read* the photographs; what are they saying to you?

Post-Reading Activity: Social Action!

For this activity, students should apply the themes of *Maus* to their own lives. Each group chooses one of the topics below and creates an in-class presentation. Encourage your students to use a variety of materials including song lyrics, pictures, videos, etc. For your convenience, a printable guide for this activity ("Action!") has been provided in the Appendix.

Stereotypes

Identify which animals are used to represent the Jews, Germans, Poles, British, French, Swedish, and Romani peoples. Why do you think the author identifies those nations with those specific animals? What is Spiegelman trying to say about stereotypes? Does he believe that they are harmful or helpful? What are some current stereotypes? How are they perpetuated? Why do think they are perpetuated? Where can they be found? Are they harmful or helpful to society? How can you challenge or encourage the notion of stereotypes?

Words & Pictures

Comics combine words and pictures. We know how to read words, but how do we "read" pictures? Look for general and specific examples of images as "text" in *Maus*. How do Spiegelman's images sometimes say more than words can? Here are some examples to consider:

What symbols are on page 33, book one? What associations do these symbols have? What is the effect of the swastika in the panels on page 33? Is it the same in every panel? Analyze other symbols in the book. We are a very visual society, and often "read" pictures rather than text. How is a picture more powerful than words? How do the media use pictures? How can we learn to read "pictures" so that we become more educated consumers?

Art's "Baggage"

We see Art carrying a satchel at various points (for instance, on pages 43, 69, and 159 of book one). What does this image suggest? What does it mean to be carrying around "baggage"? Do you think *Maus* is about dealing with baggage? If so, what kind of baggage is it? Do you carry baggage? What is it? How do you deal with the past so that it can inform your future?

People & Places

Politics change maps. Create a map of Vladek's travels during WWII. Use historical maps and sources (also see the back covers of both texts.) Where were the borders? Did the borders and city names change? When? Why? Summarize the cartographic and geopolitical changes that occurred. How do you think changing borders and city names effects people? What part does "place" or "hometown" play in identity?

Anja's Story

Some stories are never told. Art is bothered that he does not have access to his mother's story. Which story of his mother's does he tell? How does he tell it? Why does he tell it differently from his father's story? Today, what "stories" are not told? Why? How can we make sure that these stories get told?

References

Adams, K., & Petty, P. (2003). Preparing teachers for the challenge of teaching and learning with technology: Standards, strategies, and statistics. Retrieved from http://www.pearsonassessments.com/hai/images/NES_Publications/2003_06Adams_401_1.pdf

Alexander, P. A., & Fox, E. (2004). A historical perspective on reading research and practice. In R. B. Ruddel & N. J. Unrau (Eds.), *Theoretical models and processes of reading* (5th ed.) Newark, DE: International Reading Association.

Alexie, S. (2007). *The absolutely true diary of a part-time Indian*. New York: Little, Brown & Co.

Alvermann, D. E., & Hagood, M. C. (2000). Fandom and critical media literacy. *Journal of Adolescent and Adult Literacy, 43*(5), 436–446.

Alvermann, D. E., Moon, J. S., & Hagood, M. C. (1999). *Popular culture in the classroom: Teaching and researching critical media literacy*. Newark, DE: International Reading Association and the National Reading Conference.

Alvermann, D. E., & Xu, S. H. (2003). Children's everyday literacies: Intersections of popular culture and language arts instruction. *Language Arts, 81*(2), 145–155.

Aronowitz, S., & Giroux, H. (1993). *Education still under siege* (2nd ed). Westport, CT: Bergin & Garvey.

Blake, B. E., & Blake, R. W. (2005). *Literacy: Primer*. New York: Peter Lang.

Boling, E. C. (2008). Learning from teacher's conceptions of technology integration: What do blogs, instant messages, and 3D chat rooms have to do with it? *Research in the Teaching of English, 43*(1), 74–100.

Bourdieu, P. (1986). The forms of capital. In J. Richardson (Ed.), *Handbook of theory and research for the sociology of education*. New York: Greenwood.

Bourdieu, P., & Passeron, J. C. (1990). *Reproduction in education, society, and culture* (2nd ed.). Beverly Hills, CA: Sage.

Bradbury, R. (1953/1987). *Fahrenheit 451*. New York: Ballantine.

Bransford, J. D., Brown, A. L., & Cocking, R. R. (Eds.). (2000). *How people learn: Brain, mind, experience, and school.* Washington, DC: National Academies Press.

Brooks, K. (2003). Nothing sells like teen spirit: The commodification of youth culture. In K. Mallan & S. Pearce (Eds.), *Youth cultures: Texts, images, and identities.* Westport, CT: Praeger.

Browett, J. (2007). Critical literacy and visual texts: Windows on culture. Tasmania Department of Education. Retrieved from http://www.education.tas.gov.au/curriculum/standards/english/english/teachers/discussion/browett

Bruce, B. C., & Hogan, M. P. (1998). The disappearance of technology: Toward an ecological model of literacy. In D. Reinking, M. McKenna, L. Labbo, and R. Kieffer (Eds.), *Handbook of literacy and technology: Transformations in a post-typographic world* (pp. 269–281). Hillsdale, NJ: Erlbaum.

Burke, B. (1999, 2005). Antonio Gramsci, schooling and education. In *The encyclopedia of informal education.* Retrieved from http://www.infed.org/thinkers/et-gram.htm

Children's Defense Fund. (2011). *The state of America's children 2010 report.* Retrieved from http://www.childrensdefense.org/child-research-data-publications/data/state-of-americas-children-2010-report.html

Cisneros, S. (2004). *The house on Mango Street.* New York: Vintage Books.

Cope, B., & Kalantzis, M. (2000). *Multiliteracies: Literacy learning and the design of social futures.* New York: Routledge.

Crouse, J., & Trusheim, D. (1988). *The case against the SAT.* Chicago, IL: University of Chicago Press.

Cuban, L. (2003). *Oversold and underused: Computers in the classroom.* Cambridge, MA: Harvard University Press.

Darder, A., Baltodano, M., & Torres, R. (2003). Critical pedagogy: An introduction. In A. Darder, M. Baltodano, & R. Torres (Eds.), *The critical pedagogy reader.* New York: Routledge.

Delpit, L. (1995). *Other people's children: Cultural conflict in the classroom.* New York: The New Press.

Duncan-Andrade, J. M. R. (2004). Your best friend or your worst enemy: Youth popular culture, pedagogy, and curriculum in urban classrooms. *The Review of Education, Pedagogy, & Cultural Studies, 26,* 313–337. Retrieved from http://cci.sfsu.edu/files/Best%20Friend%20Worst%20Enemy.pdf

Edutopia (2011). PBL research summary: Studies validate project-based learning. Retrieved from http://www.edutopia.org/research-validates-project-based-learning

Frechette, J. D. (2002). *Developing media literacy in cyberspace: Pedagogy and critical learning for the twenty-first-century classroom.* Westport, CT: Praeger.

Freepress (2009–2012). Who owns the media? Retrieved from http://www.freepress.net/ownership/chart/

Freire, P. (1970/2000). *Pedagogy of the oppressed.* New York: Continuum.

Freire, P. (1973). *Education for critical consciousness.* New York: Continuum.

Freire, P. (1985). *The politics of education: Culture, power, and liberation.* Granby, MA: Bergin & Garvey.

Freire, P. (1998). *Teachers as cultural workers: Letters to those who dare teach.* Boulder, CO: Westview.

Freire, P. (2004). *Pedagogy of indignation.* Boulder, CO: Paradigm.

Gadotti, M. (1994). *Reading Paulo Freire: His life and work.* New York: SUNY Press.

Gainer, J. (2007). Social critique and pleasure: Critical media literacy with popular cultural texts. *Language Arts, 85*(2), 106–114.

Gay, G. (2000). *Culturally responsive teaching: Theory, research, and practice.* New York: Teachers College Press.

Gay, J. (1730/2007). *Trivia: or, the art of walking the streets of London.* Retrieved on August 7, 2012, from http://www.lulu.com/shop/john-gay/trivia-or-the-art-of-walking-the-streets-of-london/ebook/product-1861002.html.

Gee, J. P. (2007). *What video games have to teach us about learning and literacy.* New York: Palgrave.

Gee, J. P. (2008). *Social linguistics and literacies: Ideologies in discourses* (3rd ed.). New York: Routledge.

Gillan, M. M., & Gillan, J. (Eds.) (1999). *Identity lessons: Contemporary writing about learning to be American.* New York: Penguin.

Giroux, H. (1996). *Fugitive cultures: Race, violence and youth.* New York: Routledge.

Giroux, H. (2000). *Stealing innocence: Youth, corporate power, and the politics of culture.* New York: St. Martin's Press.

Golding, W. (1959/2011). *Lord of the flies.* New York: Perigee.

Goodnough, A. (2001, June 14). Strains of fourth-grade tests drive off veteran teachers, *New York Times*, p. A1.

Grossberg, L. (1994). Bringin' it all back home: Pedagogy and cultural studies. In H. Giroux & P. McLaren (Eds.), *Between borders: Pedagogy and the politics of cultural studies.* New York: Routledge.

Guzzetti, B. J., & Gamboa, M. (2004). Zines for social justice: Adolescent girls writing on their own. *Reading Research Quarterly, 39*(4), 408–436.

Hagood, M.C. (2001). Media literacies: Varied but distinguishable. *National Reading Conference Yearbook, 50,* pp. 248–261.

Herr, N. (2007). Television and health. Retrieved from *The Sourcebook for Teaching Science* on August, 7, 2012, from http://www.csun.edu/science/health/docs/tv&health.html.

Hood S., & Parker, L. (1989). Minority bias review panels and teacher testing for initial certification: A comparison of two states' efforts. *Journal of Negro Education, 58*(4), 511–519.

hooks, b. (1994*). Teaching to transgress: Education as the practice of freedom.* New York: Routledge. Retrieved from http://newlearningonline.com/literacies/chapter-6-critical-literacies/hooks-on-the-language-of-power/

Hyland, N. (2005). Being a good teacher of Black students? White teachers and unintentional racism. *Curriculum Inquiry, 35*(4), 429–459.

Institute of Education Sciences (IES). (2011). *The condition of education 2011 in brief.* Retrieved from http://nces.ed.gov/pubs2011/2011034.pdf

Jacobs, G. E. (2008). We learn what we do: Developing a repertoire of writing practices in an instant-messaging world. *Journal of Adolescent & Adult Literacy, 52*(3), 203–211.

Jewitt, C., & Kress, G. (Eds.) (2003). *Multimodal Literacy.* New York: Peter Lang.

Kellner, D. (1995). *Media culture: Cultural studies, identity, and politics between the modern and postmodern.* New York: Routledge.

Kellner, D., & Share, J. (2009). Critical media literacy, democracy, and the reconstruction of education. In S. Steinberg & D. Macedo (Eds.), *Media literacy: A reader.* New York: Peter Lang.

Kenway, J., & Bullen, E. (2001). *Consuming children.* Buckingham, U.K.: Open University Press.

Kincheloe, J. (2004). *Critical pedagogy primer* (1st ed.). New York: Peter Lang.

Kincheloe, J. (2008). *Critical pedagogy primer* (2nd ed.). New York: Peter Lang.

Kincheloe, J., Slattery, P., & Steinberg, S. (2000). *Contextualizing teaching: Introduction to education and educational foundations.* New York: Addison Wesley Longman.

Kincheloe, J., & Steinberg, S. (Eds.). (1998). *Unauthorized methods: Strategies for critical teaching.* New York: Routledge.

Kress, G. (1997). *Before writing: Rethinking paths to literacy.* London, U.K.: Routledge.

Kress, G., & Jewitt, C. (2003). *Multimodal literacy.* New York: Peter Lang.

Kress, G., & Van Leeuwen, T. (1996). *Reading images: The grammar of visual design.* London, U.K.: Routledge.

Kress, G., & Van Leeuwen, T. (2001). *Multimodal discourse.* New York: Oxford University Press.

Ladson-Billings, G. (1992). Liberatory consequences of literacy: A case of culturally relevant instruction for African American students. *Journal of Negro Education, 61,* 378–391.

Lalik, R., & Oliver, K.L. (2007). Differences and tensions in implementing a pedagogy of critical literacy with adolescent girls. *Reading Research Quarterly,* 42(1), 46–70.

Lankshear, C. (1996). Literacy studies in education: Disciplined development in a postdisciplinary age. In M. Peters (Ed.), *The emergence of cultural studies: After the disciplines.* Westport, CT: Bergin & Garvey, pp. 199–227.

Lankshear, C. (1997). *Changing literacies.* Bristol, PA: Open University Press.

Lankshear, C., & McLaren, P. (Eds.). (1993). *Critical literacy: Politics, praxis, and the postmodern.* Albany: State University of New York Press.

Lee, C. D. (2001). Is October brown Chinese? A cultural modeling activity system for underachieving students, *American Educational Research Journal, 38,* 97–141.

Linguistic Society of America (1998). Linguistics Society of America Resolution on Ebonics. In T. Perry & L. Delpit (Eds.), *The real Ebonics debate: Power, language, and the education of African American children.* Boston, MA: Beacon.

Louie, M. C. (2001, Dec. 3). The 9/11 disappeareds. *The Nation, 273*(18). Retrieved from http://www.thenation.com/article/911-disappeareds

Luke, A., Comber, B., & O'Brien, J. (1996). Critical literacies and cultural studies. In G. Bull, A. Anstey (Eds.), *The literary lexicon.* Sydney, Australia: Prentice Hall.

Mallan, K., & Pearce, S. (2003). Introduction: Tales of youth in postmodern culture. In K. Mallan & S. Pearce (Eds.), *Youth cultures: Texts, images, and identities.* Westport, CT: Praeger.

Manzo, K. K. (2001, May 16). Protests over state testing widespread. *Education Week, 20*(30), 1–26.

Marx, K. & Engels, F. (1848/1998). *The communist manifesto.* New York: Signet Classics.

McCloud, S. (1993). *Understanding comics: The invisible art.* New York: Kitchen Sink Press.

McLaren, P. (2000). *Che Guevara, Paulo Freire, and the pedagogy of revolution.* Lanham, MD: Rowman & Littlefield.

McLaren, P., Hammer, R., Sholle, D., & Reilly, S. (1995). *Rethinking media literacy: A critical pedagogy of representation.* New York: Peter Lang.

McNeil, L. (2000). Creating new inequities: Contradictions of reform. *Phi Delta Kappan, 81*(10), 729–734.

Morrell, E. (2002). Toward a critical pedagogy of popular culture: Literacy development among urban youth. *Journal of Adolescent and Adult Literacy, 46*(1), 72–78.

Na, A. (2001). *A step from heaven.* New York: Penguin.

NCTE (National Council of Teachers of English). (2011). NCTE/IRA Standards for the English Language Arts. Retrieved from http://www.ncte.org/standards

NEA (National Endowment for the Arts) (2007, November 19). National Endowment for the Arts announces new reading study. Retrieved from http://www.nea.gov/news/news07/trnr.html

Nielsen Media Research. (1998). *Report on television.* New York: Nielsen Media Research.

Nielsen. (2010). State of the media. Trends in TV viewing—2011 TV upfronts. Retrieved from http://blog.nielsen.com/nielsenwire/wp-content/uploads/2011/04/State-of-the-Media-2011-TV-Upfronts.pdf

Pahl, K., & Rowsell, J. (2005). *Literacy and education.* Thousand Oaks, CA: Paul Chapman.

Parmar, P. (2009). *Knowledge reigns supreme: The critical pedagogy of hip-hop artist KRS-ONE.* Rotterdam, Netherlands: Sense.

Parmar, P. (2010). Does hip hop have a home in urban education? In S. Steinberg (Ed.), *19 urban questions: Teaching in the city* (2nd ed.). New York: Peter Lang.

Paugh, P., Carey, J., King-Jackson, V., & Russell, S. (2007). Negotiating the literacy block: Constructing spaces for critical literacy in a high-stakes setting. *Language Arts, 85*(1), 31–42.

Perry, T., & Delpit, L. (Eds). (1998). *The real Ebonics debate: Power, language, and the education of African American children.* Boston, MA: Beacon.

Potter, W. (2005). *Media literacy* (3rd ed.). Thousand Oaks, CA: Sage.

PURE (Parents United for Responsible Education). (2007). PURE fact sheet: Bias in standardized tests. Retrieved from http://www.pureparents.org/data/files/testbias.pdf

Quint, J. (2006, May). Meeting five critical challenges of high school reform: Lessons from research on three reform models. *MDRC.* Retrieved from http://www.mdrc.org/publications/428/execsum.html

Rabinow, P. (Ed.) (1984). *The Foucault reader.* New York: Pantheon.

Rammohan, R. (2007, May 7). Advocates say standardized tests often flunk cultural bias scrutiny. Retrieved from http://news.medill.northwestern.edu/chicago/news.aspx?id=35935

Rich, M. (2008, October 8). The future of reading: Using video games as bait to hook readers. *New York Times.* Retrieved from http://www.nytimes.com/2008/10/06/books/06games.html

Richardson, W. (2008). *Blogs, wikis, podcasts and other powerful web tools for classrooms.* Thousand Oaks, CA: Corwin Press.

Ross, A. (1989). *No respect: Intellectuals and popular culture.* New York: Routledge.

Santa Ana, O. (Ed.) (2004). *Tongue-tied: The lives of multilingual children in public education.* New York: Rowman & Littlefield.

Sapphire. (1996). *Push.* New York: Knopf.

Satrapi, M. (2003). *Persepolis: The story of a childhood.* New York: Pantheon.

Saulny, S. (2005, January 19). Meaning of "proficient" varies for schools across country. *New York Times.* Retrieved from http://www.nytimes.com/2005/01/19/education/19scores.html

Schwartz, A., & Rubinstein-Avila, E. (2006). Understanding the manga hype: Uncovering the multimodality of comic-book literacies. *Journal of Adolescent and Adult Literacy, 50*(1), 40–49.

Shepherd, J. (2010, December 7). World education rankings: Which country does best at reading, maths and science? *The Guardian.* Retrieved from http://www.guardian.co.uk/news/datablog/2010/dec/07/world-educa-tion-rankings-maths-science-reading

Shepherd, J. (2010, December 7). Social class has more effect on children than good parenting, study says. *The Guardian*. Retrieved from http://www.guardian.co.uk/education/2010/dec/07/social-class-parenting-study

Silva, E. (2008, November). Measuring skills for the 21st century. Education Sector Report. Retrieved from http://www.educationsector.org/usr_doc/MeasuringSkills.pdf

Sis, P. (2007). The wall: Growing up behind the Iron Curtain. New York: Farrar, Straus & Giroux.

Smith, M. (2008). Howard Gardner, multiple intelligences and education. Retrieved from http://www.infed.org/thinkers/gardner.htm.

Smitherman, G. (1998). Black English/Ebonics: What it be like? In T. Perry & L. Delpit (Eds.), *The real Ebonics debate: Power, language, and the education of African-American children*. Boston, MA: Beacon.

Spiegelman, A. (1994, January 17). Drawing pens and politics: Mightier than the sorehead. *The Nation*, 46.

Spiegelman, A. (1997). *The complete maus: A survivor's tale*. New York: Pantheon.

Steinberg, S. (2011). Kinderculture: Mediating, simulacralizing, and pathologizing the new childhood. In S. Steinberg (Ed.), *Kinderculture: The corporate construction of childhood* (3rd ed.). Boulder, CO: Westview Press.

Storey, J. (2008). *Cultural theory and popular culture: An introduction* (4th ed.). Athens, GA: University of Georgia Press.

Street, B. (Ed.) (1993). *Cross-cultural approaches to literacy*. Cambridge, U.K.: Cambridge University Press.

Stubbs, M. (2002). Some basic sociolinguistic concepts. In L. Delpit & J. Kilgour Dowdy (Eds.), *The skin that we speak: Thoughts on language and culture in the classroom*. New York: The New Press.

Tan, S. (2006). *The arrival*. New York: Scholastic Books.

Thomas, J. W. (2000). A review of research on project-based learning. Prepared for the Autodesk Foundation. Retrieved from http://www.bie.org/research/study/review_of_project_based_learning_2000

Trudeau, M. (2010, December 20). Video games boost brain power, multitasking skills. *National Public Radio*. Retrieved from http://www.npr.org/2010/12/20/132077565/video-games-boost-brain-power-multitasking-skills

United Press International (2008, November 19). U.S. slipping in education rankings. Retrieved from http://www.upi.com/Top_News/2008/11/19/US-slipping-in-education-rankings/UPI-90221227104776/

USA Today (2010, December 7). In ranking, U.S. students trail global leaders. Retrieved from http://www.usatoday.com/news/education/2010-12-07-us-students-international-ranking_N.htm

Weaver, J. (2009). *Popular culture primer* (Rev. ed.). New York: Peter Lang.

Weaver, J. (2012, July 24). Teens tune out TV, log on instead. *Msnbc.com*. Retrieved from http://www.msnbc.msn.com/id/3078614/ns/technology_and_science-tech_and_gadgets/t/teens-tune-out-tv-log-instead/#.UCFeS02PXVQ.

Weaver, S. (1984). The emergence of dialectical theory: Philosophy and political inquiry. Chicago: University of Chicago Press.

Weisburgh, M. (2007, October 3). U.S. education compared to other developed nations. Retrieved from http://academicbiz.typepad.com/piloted/2007/10/us-education-co.html

Weiss, M. J., & Weiss, H. S. (Eds.). (2002). *Big city cool: Short stories about urban youth*. New York: Persea.

West, K. C. (2008). Weblogs and literary response: Socially situated identities and hybrid social languages in English class blogs. *Journal of Adolescent and Adult Literacy*, 51(7), 588–598.

White House Council on Women & Girls. (2011). *Women in America: Indicators of social and economic well-being*. Retrieved from http://www.whitehouse.gov/sites/default/files/rss_viewer/Women_in_America.pdf

Williams, B. T. (2008). "Tomorrow will not be like today": Literacy and identity in a world of multiliteracies. *Journal of Adolescent and Adult Literacy*, 51(8), 682–686.

Williams, R. (2006). The analysis of culture. In J. Storey, (Ed.) *Cultural theory and popular culture: A reader* (3rd ed.) London, U.K.: Pearson Education.

Willis, P. (1977). *Learning to labor: How working class kids get working class jobs*. New York: Columbia University Press.

Zinn, H. (2005). *A People's History of the United States*.New York: Harper Perennial.

Appendix

WORLD POWER PLAYS

Name: _____

STEP 1: Choose a Political System

Brainstorm a list of the major political systems found in the modern world. Select a political system to explore: _____

In your own words, define the political system you selected.

_____

_____

_____

_____

_____

_____

STEP 2: Explore a Country

Choose a country in which your political system is currently practiced. Summarize the history of the political system in that country. Describe the day-to-day experience of people living in that country.

_____

_____

_____

_____

_____

_____

_____

_____

_____

SCHOOL SOCIAL PYRAMID

In the pyramid below, create dividing lines to indicate your school's social hierarchy.

POWER WALK

Name: _____

   In this activity, you will be a photojournalist documenting the condition of the NYC subway system. You will begin at the subway stop closest to your home and visit stations across the city. To document the conditions, notice the garbage cans (Are they overflowing or tidy?), the walls (Are the billboards in good condition? Is there artwork? Is there an LCD train schedule?), and the floors and train tracks (Are the floors clean? Are the tracks clear? Is there an elevator?). If you have a camera, take pictures. Use the subway rides between stations to record your observations in the chart below.

SUBWAY STOP	GENERAL DESCRIPTION	GARBAGE CANS	WALLS	FLOORS/TRACKS/STAIRS/ELEVATOR
My subway stop:				
66th Street (1 train to the Upper West Side)				
Jackson Avenue (4 train to the South Bronx)				
Seneca Avenue (M train to Queens)				

Did you discover any discrepancies in how the subway stations are maintained? Explain.

POWER WALK

Name: _____

In this activity, you will be documenting the condition of your local community. You will begin in the area closest to your home and then visit different landmarks or neighborhoods within your community.

To document the conditions, notice the garbage cans (Are they overflowing or tidy?) and the walls (Are the billboards in good condition? What products are advertised on these billboards? Is there graffiti on buildings or storefronts?), and houses, stores, sidewalks, and roads (Are the houses built well or well landscaped? Are local clothing and food stores well maintained and structurally sound? What restaurants are in your area? What are the names of the stores and restaurants? Are they locally owned or national chains? Are sidewalks clean and well maintained? Are roads smooth, clear, and free of pot-holes?). If you have a camera, take pictures.

COMMUNITY	GENERAL DESCRIPTION	GARBAGE CANS	WALLS	HOUSES, STORES, RESTAURANTS	ROADS & SIDEWALKS
My street address					
3–5 blocks away from my home					
5–10 blocks away from my home					

Report the findings. What did you discover on your power walk?

THE ROAD TO ME

Name: _____

Graduate from high school

MY GOALS:

WHERE IS SHE NOW?

YEAR: _____

Describe Precious' HOME: _____
_____
_____
_____

Describe Precious' HEALTH: _____
_____
_____
_____
_____
_____

Describe Precious' FINANCIAL STATUS: _____
_____
_____
_____
_____

OTHER DETAILS: _____
_____
_____
_____
_____
_____
_____

MY AMERICA

1. What images are commonly associated with America?

    _____

    _____

2. Reflect on these images. (Have you ever eaten apple pie? Do you own a pickup truck? Have you ever seen a bald eagle?)

    _____

    _____

3. Is the America you see on television, in the movies, in magazines, the America you live in? Why or why not?

    _____

    _____

    _____

4. What does your America look like?

    _____

    _____

5. What does being an American mean to you?

    _____

    _____

6. Draw your American symbol:

INTERPRETING THE AMERICAN DREAM

1. What is the American dream? _____
_____

2. How is it depicted in the media? _____
_____
_____

3. Do you believe that everyone shares the same dream? If so, what is it? _____
_____
_____
_____

4. Are you living the American dream? Why or why not? _____
_____
_____

Compare & Contrast

Part 2: Read "The New Colossus"
Where is this poem inscribed? Why? _____
_____
_____

How did Emma Lazarus view America?
_____
_____
_____

Did she have an American dream? If so, what was it? _____
_____
_____
_____

Part 3: Read "There are tens of thousands of poems on these walls"
Where is this poem inscribed? Why?
_____
_____
_____

How did the writer view America?_____
_____
_____

Did the writer have an American dream? If so, what was it?_____
_____
_____

HERITAGE PROJECT

PHASE 1: RESEARCHING
The first step in the Heritage Project is research. This includes conducting family interviews and searching various historical databases like www.ellisisland.org for information. After gathering some information on your family's heritage, particularly the immigration experience, choose someone in your family to interview.

I will interview: _____

Interview questions:

    1. _____

    2. _____

    3. _____

PHASE 2: ANALYZING
The second step in the Heritage Project is analysis. This means analyzing all the information that you've collected. You should be able to identify major points in your family's narrative. For example:

    1. When did your family first arrive to the U.S.? _____

_____

    2. What was their country of origin? _____

    3. Why did they decide to immigrate? _____

_____

_____

PHASE 3: REPORTING
The final stage of the Heritage Project is reporting what you've discovered. Create a multimedia presentation with pictures and maps. You can even use clips from family videos and interviews.

I AM...ME?

In the speech bubbles below, describe each poet's struggle with identity.

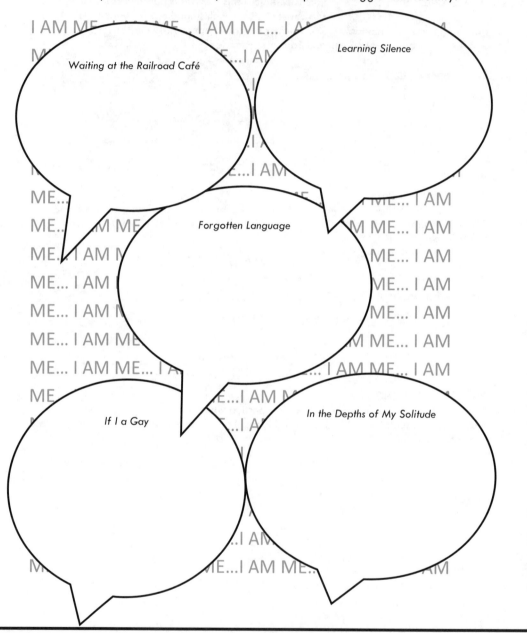

DEBUNKING THE WESTERN MYTH

	Understanding the Myth [watch clip from a popular Western]	Debunking the Myth [watch clip from *500 Nations*]
When was this film made?		
Who produced this film?		
Who is the intended audience for this film?		
How are Native Americans depicted in this film? Why?		
How are non–Native Americans depicted in this film? Why?		
How does this film support or debunk the Western myth?		

LOCATION, LOCATION, LOCATION

Compare and contrast how setting impacts the narrative.

THE CHAPTERS OF MY LIFE

"I make a story for my life for each step my brown shoe takes" (Esperanza in *The House on Mango Street*)

Title: _____

This book is dedicated to: _____

Table of Contents:

Chapter 1: _____

Chapter 2: _____

Chapter 3: _____

Chapter 4: _____

Chapter 5: _____

Chapter 6: _____

Chapter 7: _____

Chapter 8: _____

Chapter 9: _____

Chapter 10: _____

Chapter 11: _____

Chapter 12: _____

Chapter 13: _____

Chapter 14: _____

Chapter 15: _____

TAKE A TOUR OF MY NEIGHBORHOOD

Your neighborhood is being included in a new travel guide! Because you're a local expert, the publisher has asked you to suggest attractions and activities.

MY NEIGHBORHOOD: _____

GETTING THERE & AWAY: Transportation

PLACES TO SEE: Attractions

PLACES TO EAT: Restaurants

THINGS TO DO: Activities

PEOPLE TO MEET: Important Individuals

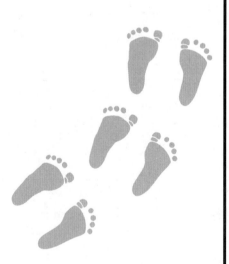

THINGS TO AVOID: Nuisances

IT'S A HARD THING GROWING UP...

As your group reads through the poems, explore the following questions and fill in the graphic organizer below:

POEM	SPEAKER Who is the speaker in the poem?	CONFLICT What conflict is the speaker referring to in the poem?	WARTIME EXPERIENCE How did the speaker experience the war? How did the war shape the speaker's life?

K	W	L
What I Know	What I Want to Know	What I've Learned

PERSEPOLIS & THE WALL

In the chart below, compare and contrast Marjane Satrapi's Persepolis to Peter Sis' The Wall

	PERSEPOLIS	THE WALL
What are the political beliefs of the authors' parents?		
How do both regimes acquire and retain power?		
How are the children of the regimes indoctrinated?		
How does each of the governments deal with insurgency?		
How do the authors view Western culture?		
What role do the arts play in both authors' lives?		
How do the authors resist the authorities?		
What is the current government in both countries?		
How does Marji's story reflect her experience as a young woman while Peter's story reflects his experience as a young man?		
Why do you think Czechoslovakia eventually became a democracy while Iran has not?		

BURNING BOOKS

When Fahrenheit 451 was reprinted in 1967, the publishers created a special edition to be sold in high schools. Without informing Bradbury or putting a note in the edition, the publisher removed all "bad" words from the novel. The expurgated edition was sold for 13 years before a friend of Bradbury's alerted him to the changes. Eventually, the publisher withdrew the censored version and replaced it with the original. The publicity generated by this incident caused the American Library Association's Intellectual Freedom Committee to investigate other school books and use its considerable economic clout to warn publishers that any excised versions of books must be clearly identified.

1. How do you feel about books? _____
   _____

2. What are some materials that you like to read? _____
   _____
   _____

3. Why do you think someone would want to challenge or ban a book? _____
   _____
   _____

4. Can a book be dangerous? To whom? How? _____
   _____
   _____

5. How do you feel about censorship? Is it ever justified? Explain. _____
   _____
   _____

6. Why would a government encourage censorship? _____
   _____
   _____

7. In your opinion, what role do books play in society? _____
   _____
   _____

8. In your opinion, do offensive books play a role in society? Explain. _____
   _____
   _____
   _____

CODA

This coda was published in the 50th anniversary edition of Ray Bradbury's Fahrenheit 451(© 1979 Ray Bradbury).[*]

About two years ago, a letter arrived from a solemn young Vassar lady telling me how much she enjoyed reading my experiment in space mythology, *The Martian Chronicles.* But, she added, wouldn't it be a good idea, this late in time, to rewrite the book inserting more women's characters and roles?

A few years before that I got a certain amount of mail concerning the same Martian book complaining that the blacks in the book were Uncle Toms and why didn't I "do them over"? Along about then came a note from a Southern white suggesting that I was prejudiced in favor of the blacks and the entire story should be dropped.

Two weeks ago my mountain of mail delivered forth a pipsqueak mouse of a letter from a well-known publishing house that wanted to reprint my story "The Fog Horn" in a high school reader. In my story, I had described a lighthouse as having, late at night, an illumination coming from it that was a "God-Light." Looking up at it from the view-point of any sea-creature one would have felt that one was in "the Presence."

The editors had deleted "God-Light" and "in the Presence."

Some five years back, the editors of yet another anthology for school readers put together a volume with some 400 (count 'em) short stories in it. How do you cram 400 short stories by Twain, Irving, Poe, Maupassant and Bierce into one book?

Simplicity itself. Skin, debone, demarrow, scarify, melt, render down and destroy. Every adjective that counted, every verb that moved, every metaphor that weighed more than a mosquito—out! Every simile that would have made a sub-moron's mouth twitch—gone! Any aside that explained the two-bit philosophy of a first-rate writer—lost!

Every story, slenderized, starved, bluepenciled, leeched and bled white, resembled every other story. Twain read like Poe read like Shakespeare read like Dostoevsky read like—in the finale—Edgar Guest. Every word of more than three syllables had been razored. Every image that demanded so much as one instant's attention—shot dead.

Do you begin to get the damned and incredible picture?

How did I react to all of the above?

By "firing" the whole lot.
By sending rejection slips to each and every one. By ticketing the assembly of idiots to the far reaches of hell.

The point is obvious. There is more than one way to burn a book. And the world is full of people running about with lit matches. Every minority, be it Baptist / Unitarian, Irish / Italian / Octogenarian / Zen Buddhist, Zionist/Seventh -day Adventist, Women's Lib/ Republican, Mattachine/ Four Square Gospel feels it has the will, the right, the duty to douse the kerosene, light the fuse. Every dimwit editor who sees himself as the source of all dreary blanc-mange plain porridge unleavened literature, licks his guillotine and eyes the neck of any author who dares to speak above a whisper or write above a nursery rhyme.
Fire-Captain Beatty, in my novel *Fahrenheit 451*, described how the books were burned first by minorities, each ripping a page or a paragraph from this book, then that, until the day came when the books were empty and the minds shut and the libraries closed forever.

---

[*]Bradbury, R. (1953/1979). *Fahrenheit 451*. New York: Ballantine.

"Shut the door, they're coming through the window, shut the window, they're coming through the door," are the words to an old song. They fit my life-style with newly arriving butcher/censors every month. Only six weeks ago, I discovered that, over the years, some cubby-hole editors at Ballantine Books, fearful of contaminating the young, had, bit by bit, censored some 75 separate sections from the novel. Students, reading the novel which, after all, deals with censorship and book-burning in the future, wrote to tell me of this exquisite irony. Judy-Lynn Del Rey, one of the new Ballantine editors, is having the entire book reset and republished this summer with all the damns and hells back in place.

A final test for old Job II here: I sent a play, *Leviathan 99*, off to a university theater a month ago. My play is based on the "Moby Dick" mythology, dedicated to Melville, and concerns a rocket crew and a blind space captain who venture forth to encounter a Great White Comet and destroy the destroyer. My drama premieres as an opera in Paris this autumn.

But, for now, the university wrote back that they hardly dared do my play—it had no women in it! And the ERA ladies on campus would descend with ball-bats if the drama department even tried!

Grinding my bicuspids into powder, I suggested that would mean, from now on, no more productions of *Boys in the Band* (no women), or *The Women* (no men). Or, counting heads, male and female, a good lot of Shakespeare that would never be seen again, especially if you count lines and find that all the good stuff went to the males!

I wrote back maybe they should do my play one week, and *The Women* the next. They probably thought I was joking, and I'm not sure that I wasn't.

For it is a mad world and it will get madder if we allow the minorities, be they dwarf or giant, orangutan or dolphin, nuclear-head or water-conversationalist, pro-computerologist or Neo-Luddite, simpleton or sage, to interfere with aesthetics. The real world is the playing ground for each and every group, to make or unmake laws. But the tip of the nose of my book or stories or poems is where their rights end and my territorial imperatives begin, run and rule. If Mormons do not like my plays, let them write their own. If the Irish hate my Dublin stories, let them rent type-writers. If teachers and grammar school editors find my jawbreaker sentences shatter their mushmilk teeth, let them eat stale cake dunked in weak tea of their own ungodly manufacture. If the Chicano intellectuals wish to re-cut my "Wonderful Ice Cream Suit" so it shapes "Zoot," may the belt unravel and the pants fall.

For, let's face it, digression is the soul of wit. Take philosophic asides away from Dante, Milton or Hamlet's father's ghost and what stays is dry bones. Laurence Sterne said it once: Digressions, incontestably, are the sunshine, the life, the soul of reading! Take them out and one cold eternal winter would reign in every page. Restore them to the writer—he steps forth like a bridegroom, bids them all-hail, brings in variety and forbids the appetite to fail.

In sum, do not insult me with the beheadings, finger-choppings or the lung-defiations you plan for my works. I need my head to shake or nod, my hand to wave or make into a fist, my lungs to shout or whisper with. I will not go gently onto a shelf, degutted, to become a non-book.

All you umpires, back to the bleachers. Referees, hit the showers. It's my game. I pitch, I hit, I catch. I run the bases. At sunset I've won or lost. At sunrise, I'm out again, giving it the old try. And no one can help me. Not even you.

REVIEW QUESTIONS

1. What does it mean that "there is more than one way to burn a book"? _____
_____
_____

2. How does Bradbury define "minorities"? _____
_____
_____

3. In Bradbury's opinion, why would minorities want to ban a book? _____
_____
_____

4. Why do you think the university refused to put on Bradbury's play? Do you agree with their
decision? Why or why not? _____
_____
_____

5. What does Bradbury advise minorities who disagree with his work? _____
_____
_____

6. What are "beheadings, finger-choppings, [and] lung-deflations" symbolic of? _____
_____
_____

7. What does Bradbury mean when he says, "I will not go gently onto the shelf, degutted, to
become a non-book." Who is degutting? And what does it mean for a book to become a
"non-book"? _____
_____
_____

8. How does Bradbury define the purpose of books? Do you agree or disagree with him? ___
_____
_____

9. In the last paragraph, what "game" is Bradbury referring to? Who are the "umpires" and
"referees"? _____
_____
_____

TAKE A TV BREAK!

The average American teen spends watches about 24 hours of TV a week (Nielsen, 2010). Where do you fit in?

How many hours of TV do you normally watch a day?

☐ 6-8 hours   ☐ 3-5 hours   ☐ 1-3 hours   ☐ None

How do you watch TV?

☐ Alone   ☐ with friends   ☐ with family   ☐ Other

How many TVs are in your household?

☐ 4 or more   ☐ 2-4   ☐ 1   ☐ None

What are your favorite TV shows? (Check all that apply.)

☐ Reality TV   ☐ Comedy   ☐ Drama   ☐ Games

Where do you watch TV?

☐ Home   ☐ Cell Phone   ☐ Computer   ☐ Other

Where does TV fit into your priorities? (Place a number in each box; 1 being the least important and 5 being the most.)

☐ TV   ☐ Homework   ☐ Friends   ☐ Family

UNDERSTANDING MAUS

Read the excerpt from an interview given by the author, and then answer the questions below.

"Maus, my comic book about my parents' life in Hitler's Europe, which uses cats to represent Germans and mice to represent Jews, was made in collaboration with Hitler. (Now will I have to share my Pulitzer?) It was the Nazis' idea to divvy the human race up into species, into *Übermenschen* and *Untermenschen*, to "exterminate" (as opposed to murder) Jews like vermin, to use Zyklon B—a pesticide—in the gas chambers. My anthropomorphized mice carry trace elements of Fips's anti-Semitic Jew-as-rat cartoons for *Der Stürmer*, but by being particularized they are invested with personhood; they stand upright and affirm their humanity. Cartoons personalize; they give specific form to stereotypes."!

QUESTIONS:

1. What does the author means when he says *Maus* was written in "collaboration with Hitler" _____
   _____
   _____

2. Who are the *Übermenschen* and *Untermenschen*? _____
   _____
   _____
   _____

3. Are people comparable to rodents and bugs? Explain. _____
   _____
   _____

4. The author decides to make the mice personable and give them a sense of humanity. How does he do this? Is he successful? Why or why not? _____
   _____
   _____
   _____
   _____

ACTION!

For this activity, you will apply the themes of Maus to your own life. Each group should choose one of the topics below to create an in-class presentation. Draw inspiration from Maus and include a variety of materials like music, photography, and film to create your presentation.

- **Stereotypes**

  Identify which animals are used to represent the Jews, Germans, Poles, British, French, Swedish, and Romani peoples. Why do you think the author identifies those nations with those specific animals? What is Spiegelman trying to say about stereotypes? Does he believe that they are harmful or helpful? What are some current stereotypes? How are they perpetuated? Why do you think they are perpetuated? Where can they be found? Are they harmful or helpful to society? How can you challenge or encourage the notion of stereotypes?

- **Words & Pictures**

  Comics combine words and pictures. We know how to read words, but how do we "read" pictures? Look for general and specific examples of images as "text" in *Maus*. How do Spiegelman's images sometimes say more than words can? Here are some examples to consider: What symbols are on page 33? What associations do these symbols have? What is the affect of the swastika in the panels on page 33? Is it the same in every panel? Analyze other symbols in the book. We are a very visual society, and often "read" pictures rather than text. How is a picture more powerful than words? How do the media use pictures? How can we learn to read "pictures" so that we become more educated consumers?

- **Art's "Baggage"**

  We see Art carrying a satchel at various points (for instance, on pages 43, 69, and 159 of book one). What does this image suggest? What does it mean to be carrying around "baggage"? Do you think *Maus* is about dealing with baggage? If so, what kind of baggage is it? Do you carry baggage? What is it? How do you deal with the past so that it can inform your future?

- **People & Places**

  Politics change maps. Create a map of Vladek's travels during World War II. Use historical maps and sources (also see the back covers of both texts.) Where were the borders? Did the borders and city names change? When? Why? Summarize the cartographic and geopolitical changes that occurred. How do you think changing borders and city names affects people? What part does "place" or "hometown" play in identity?

- **Anja's Story**

  Some stories are never told. Art is bothered that he does not have access to his mother's story. Which story of his mother's does he tell? How does he tell it? Why does he tell it differently from his father's story? Today, what "stories" are not told? Why? How can we make sure that these stories get told?

Critical Literacy/Critical Textual Analysis Guide Sheet

Deconstructing the text: This helps students understand who or what is represented or underrepresented in the text. Ask students to think about representation, misrepresentation, and underrepresentation of different groups based on: race, class, gender, culture, ethnicity, sexuality, ability, age/peer groups, and physical appearance.

- Whose voices are represented in the text?
- What does this representation mean to me? And to others?
- Which "groups" are represented in the text? How are they represented?
- Does this representation reflect my "group" (peer group, class, race, ethnicity, gender, sexuality, ability level, etc.) fairly or accurately?
- How are these depictions or representations (of the group) formed? Where does it come from? The author? Society? Media?
- Through whose perspective (or eyes) is the text telling the story?
- Whose voices are excluded from the text?

Reconstructing the text: This helps students understand the inherent biases found within the text and allows them to analyze content through multiple perspectives. Reconstruct the text by replacing certain elements of the text based on race, class, gender, age, setting, or theme.

- Change the *sex* of the main characters (or any characters) to determine if the meaning changes in any way. Consider changing heterosexual characters to LGBT (lesbian, gay, bisexual, or transgendered) characters and vice versa.
- Change the *race, class, ethnicity, or age* of the characters to determine if the meaning changes. Ask students to think about how characters would be described and depicted if any of these elements were to change. How would the overall story change?
- Change the *setting of the story* to a different time, place, or social class. How would the story differ in meaning if the setting took place in an urban, suburban, or rural environment? How would the story change if it took place in medieval, modern, or contemporary times?
- Change the major or obvious *theme(s)* of the story and replace with opposite theme(s). Allow students to change themes in the story so they are able to connect personally with the characters and content. Discuss how this changes the outcome of the story and author's intent.

CriticalLiteracy/Critical Textual Analysis Guide Sheet

What can we do? Praxis—Taking Action! If students are compelled enough, teachers should provide opportunities for students to take action to address a problem or issue they feel is unjust in their school, community, or larger society.

- ***In School:*** Do students have decision-making power in creation of classroom or school rules, curriculum development, or lesson planning with teacher? Is there student government in place? If so, what is their role when school policies and curricula are decided upon? Do students have voice in creating the lunch menu or after-school clubs? Is there a student newspaper? Is there student-led news reporting where students report or make important announcements through a public address system in the morning or at designated times during the school day? Can students create multimedia messages (i.e., filming a Public Service Announcement (PSA), video, or documentary) that can be played for all students in the school? Can students write, produce, and direct a play (performance arts) on select themes that will be presented to the entire school? Can students create murals on school walls? Because many students are attracted and highly engaged in technological devices, how can we utilize their strengths in this area to address social injustices? Can students create websites? Electronic newsletters? Social networking websites limited to only members of their school or community?

- ***In Community:*** What are the issues affecting your local community? How can we create awareness and provide resolution to these issues? How are local community organizations collaborating with the students and school? How do we encourage parents to get involved? Who are our local politicians and how can we work with them to improve conditions in our community? Invite these representatives to our school or other community venue. How can we involve the police department to improve the relationship between youth, community members, and the police? Can we engage in local food drives or fundraising activities that will benefit our community?

- ***In Society:*** Who are the state and federal politicians representing us? Contact these representatives through use of technology. Students can engage in protests and boycotts against organizations, social or political causes, or consumer products. They can engage in letter-writing campaigns or petitions sent to local or state authorities, newspapers' editorial sections, or media corporations. This can be accomplished electronically (email) or through hard copy.